BAPTISM IS NOT ENOUGH

BAPTISM IS NOT ENOUGH

How Understanding God's Covenant
Explains Everything

John G. Crawford

canonpress
Moscow, Idaho

Published by Canon Press
P.O. Box 8729, Moscow, Idaho 83843
800.488.2034 | www.canonpress.com

Cover design by James Engerbretson.
Interior design by Valerie Anne Bost.

Library of Congress Cataloging-in-Publication Data
Crawford, John G., author.
Baptism is not enough : how understanding God's covenant explains everything / John G. Crawford.
Second edition. | Moscow, Idaho : Canon Press, 2022. |
   Includes bibliographical references.
LCCN 2022025729 | ISBN 9781957905167 (paperback)
LCSH: Covenants—Religious aspects—Christianity. | Covenant theology.
Classification: LCC BT155 .C74 2022 | DDC 231.7/6—dc23/eng/20221104
LC record available at https://lccn.loc.gov/2022025729

22 23 24 25 26 27 28 29   10 9 8 7 6 5 4 3 2 1

To Cade, Lachlan, Aila, and Paisley.
Bound to Christ.

CONTENTS

FOREWORD

A NUMBER OF YEARS AGO, A BAPTIST FRIEND accused our church of cultivating a covenantal buzzword culture. He thought we were simply using the word covenant as an all-purpose adjective, one helpful in describing absolutely everything around us. The example he used, as I recall, was our covenant peanut butter and covenant jelly.

This abuse can happen, but even when it isn't happening, it can sometimes look as though it is happening. But why?

The reason this happens is that we do not take the time to define what a covenant actually is. We are usually not this sloppy with other key biblical terms—words like justification, or atonement, or imputation, or sanctification. We define these terms, taking the sweep of all biblical history into account, and then we remember how we have defined them. There are problems that can arise with this as well, but overall, it is good and helps keep things clear.

We are not nearly this careful with the word covenant. And this is truly odd. Think about this for a moment. Our Bible is divided into two major sections—the Old Testament (covenant) and the New Testament (covenant). What would many Christians do if a non-Christian friend noticed that fact and said, "You know, that really puzzles me. What is a covenant anyhow?" In too many cases, the Christian would be reduced to explaining how an old covenant is a collection of books that begins with Genesis and ends with Malachi, while a new covenant begins with Matthew.

A covenant is a forensic or legal arrangement that establishes a defined relationship. The relationship that is defined is a relationship between persons, so that we must not think of this definition as being rigid, legalistic, or impersonal. One of our best illustrations of a covenant in the modern day—because it is still functioning, although under assault—is the covenant of marriage. Our modern confusions about covenant have had far-reaching and destructive consequences.

In this book, John Crawford does a very good job in beginning his discussion of infant baptism by discussing and defining (from the Scriptures) what a covenant is. He does this thoroughly in the first portion of the book, and some readers might be tempted to check the cover of the book from time to time. They thought they were getting a book about infant baptism, and here it is chapter 3 and still no water, and still no babies.

But the reason for this is straightforward. Crawford states in this book that Paul Jewett's book on baptism is the best credo-baptist [believer's baptism] case out there—and this is a sentiment with which I agree. When I was going through the turmoil of my own transition on this subject, I read a stack of books, and in my judgment, Jewett's was the best representation of the credo-baptist position. And in that book, he points out why Crawford's approach is a very wise approach for the paedo-baptist [baptism of children] to take.

If a brand-new Christian wants to decide what to think about the subject of baptism, he can get a concordance or Bible search software, and look up all the instances of baptism in the New Testament. It seems simple. In the book of Acts, everyone professes faith first, and gets baptized second. Why is there even a debate about this? But Jewett wrote that if we expand our discussion to include things like generations, and olive trees, and covenants, the paedo-baptist case becomes, to use Jewett's word for it, a juggernaut.

I do not commend this approach for pragmatic reasons. I commend it because it is the fastest way for modern individualists to learn an intellectual framework that is generally alien to us, and which ought not to be alien to us. That framework is a covenantal one, and is pervasive throughout Scripture. I commend this book to you as a good help in restoring this framework.

DOUGLAS WILSON

INTRODUCTION

IN THE SUMMER OF 1995 I READ A CHRISTIAN socialist book that changed my life. It was Ron Sider's *Rich Christians in an Age of Hunger.* I read it more than once and was convinced that all professing Christians should read this work and begin to conduct themselves according to the agenda found within it. Now before you put this book down, let me first tell you why Sider's book changed my life. Its impact came from the fact that it unapologetically connected my Christian faith with the world around me. It went beyond the first step of "soul-winning" to "culture changing" according to the Word of God. In a world where Christianity did not often venture much beyond a person's internal "relationship with God" or outside the four walls of the church, it was a breath of fresh air. Of course we as Christians would fight cultural battles around us when they were hot issues, such as abortion, homosexuality, or—a favorite of the last two centuries—alcohol, but we did not take a comprehensive approach to the application of God's Word to every area of the world around us. I was beside myself with excitement that Sider's book did.

An interesting thing happened not long after the experience described above. I read a refutation of Sider's book. It was David Chilton's *Productive Christians in an Age of Guilt Manipulators*. Those not familiar with the importance and function of good rhetoric may have been put off by the book. But good confrontational rhetoric is quite beneficial. It is especially useful for those sitting outside looking in on an ideological debate. It helps them evaluate and find holes in any given argument. In short, it aids in decision-making, understanding, refining and solidifying ideas, and, ultimately, in gaining direction that manifests itself in the way they conduct themselves throughout life. In this way healthy debate becomes essential to progress in thinking and therefore everything else.

So what was so helpful about this particular refutation of Sider's book? Beginning with the same premise that Scripture did in fact apply to every area of life, Chilton remained fully faithful to God's Word and consistent with its authority and the complete sovereignty of God. As opposed to Scripture not applying to all of life or only some of Scripture applying to all of life (Sider's view), his book was helpful in driving home that all Scripture applies to all of life. As such it became a jumping-off point for scouring Scripture and reevaluating all of my presuppositions in light of God's sovereignty as well as *sola scriptura* (Scripture alone) and *tota scriptura* (all of Scripture).

After digging deeper into the Bible and probably 20,000 pages of discussion from past centuries through contemporary debates, I found myself in a much different place. It was a place where God was truly sovereign and the scope of His purpose for the world was all-encompassing.

That brings us to this book. The original title of this book was *Covenant Representation and Infant Baptism*, but after finishing a draft of the manuscript it was apparent that the title did not do it justice. The original impetus for writing the book arose out of a decision to move my membership to a new church. Holding a doctrine of infant baptism would not allow me to continue membership in a Baptist church.

While this may not be such a big deal to most people, it was for me. I had been in the fellowship for over thirty years; it was a large church, one in which my father had been pastor for all of those years. This was a community who, although they did not give full attention to covenant theology, helped form who I am, led by a father and pastor who fostered the understanding of the supremacy of the Bible and the ideal of living with integrity according to it and one's own convictions.

It was my father who knew me well enough and was perceptive enough to say, "There seems to be more here than just the issue of baptism at work." He was right—there was. Baptism was an immensely important issue, but it did not stand on its own. It was merely one facet of a unified and comprehensive paradigm. So, perhaps like many other books that are written, I wrote this short book out of necessity.

The good news is that we are seeing a return to the Reformation's insistence on the absolute sovereignty of God. Going beyond this though, its emphasis on covenantal representation could clear up many difficulties in the debate of infant baptism in Reformed Baptist circles. In addition, a covenantal approach to our families and the gospel will provide necessary traction to the many who are giving their all to carry the name of Jesus Christ around the world.

The ideas in this book are not new. When you think you have new ideas and go to put them on paper you realize most everything has already been written. All there is to offer is a new presentation from a unique perspective perhaps to a different audience with a few changes at the margin. I do this, hoping to extend ideas that need to be embraced as the church continues her victorious journey through history.

I used the term "all-encompassing" above. That is what this book seeks to point out. God's purpose for His people covers all of life. Biblical Christianity is truly a comprehensive paradigm. It touches everything. God is transcendent, but He also relates to us; and He relates to us not only inside of us or just through the life of our church but He relates to the whole created order for His glory. He does this through the covenant.

The purpose of this book is not necessarily to change the doctrine of the reader, although for some I hope it does. For a number of reasons people do not easily change doctrinally. There are many who have not worked out their first principles or presuppositions, and it is to those whom this work may be of some benefit.

I was recently reading on the website of a church local to my area, "We simply offer a relationship with Jesus free from rules, rituals, or religion, empowered through the Holy Spirit." This statement is neither logically nor theologically sound, as this book will demonstrate. God relates to His creation through covenant. His covenant addresses all of life. It is all-encompassing. It connects everything to everything. As Cornelius Van Til stated, "There is not a place in all the universe where man can go and say this is my private realm. No button he can press and say here I step outside of God's jurisdiction. If man had such a button he would always have his finger on it. But it does not exist. He only lives, moves, and has his being in God's world."[1] Or Abraham Kuyper: "... there is not a square inch in the whole domain of our human existence over which Christ, who is Sovereign over all, does not cry: 'Mine!'"[2]

It wasn't my doctrine of baptism that changed first and foremost. It was my doctrine of God's covenant with His created order. The people around me who saw changes in my faith and wondered, "Why?," deserve a complete answer. This book is an attempt at an answer.

1. From a lecture by Rousas J. Rushdoony, "The Birth of the New Christian Order": https://pocketcollege.com/transcript/RR266A2.html.
2. Abraham Kuyper, "Sphere Sovereignty" in James D. Bratt, *Abraham Kuyper: A Centennial Reader* (Grand Rapids: Eerdmans, 1998), 488.

CHAPTER ONE:
WHAT IS A COVENANT?

FROM A YOUNG AGE I WAS TAUGHT THAT the most important thing in life was my relationship with God. Much of this book is designed to drive home that very idea. The question is, what does that relationship look like?

What is the nature of that relationship and how are we to conduct our daily life accordingly? Is it a mystical connection to a transcendent God? Is it a daily response to my conscience? What does it mean to have a "close" or a "good" relationship?

A host of evangelical clichés surround these questions but they do not provide the clear insight needed to deal with such important matters. The answer to these questions and many more are bound up in the scriptural idea of a covenant. In fact, from a biblical standpoint, the very key to understanding our relationship to God is the covenant. Most Christians would acknowledge that the issue is not really whether we have a relationship with God or not, since we all do. We were all created by the Triune God, in His image and for His good pleasure. As created beings we are linked to our Creator. Our very existence depends on Him.

The question is not, therefore, whether we relate to God, but how. How do we relate in time and space to a supernatural God? Since creation, God has related to man through covenants. These covenants provide a real-world structure through which we relate to God on earth.

So what is a covenant? In a biblical sense, it is a legal bond between two or more parties—"legal" meaning that each party makes a statement (confession) and agrees to specific terms, with consequences invoked on each party for failure to keep the terms. This agreement takes place in the presence of witnesses and is usually followed by the public "sealing" or display of the agreement and sometimes a meal together. The parties then relate within the context of this formal structure. Relating together within this legal bond is referred to as being "in covenant" with one another. The parties are connected through this legal bond. The bond is not one of being materially connected in any way. Neither is it of a magical or mystical connection unseen in Scripture. It is a legal connection.

Why then is this so important to understand? Because this is how God chose to link the unseen to the seen, the supernatural to the material or created order here on earth. This in no way diminishes the role of the Holy Spirit and His work within the hearts of men. It merely gives outward manifestation to the power of God's Spirit.[1] It is also important to note that this is in direct opposition to some mystical religions, which reject a Creator in favor of the sovereignty of man and nature. They view the connection with God as a chain of being throughout all things. The Christian confesses a wholly separate, sovereign God that is over His creation. He chose to relate to this creation through covenant.

COVENANT AT CREATION

We are all under the covenant at creation because we are all sons of the first Adam. When God created Adam He related to him on certain terms. He asserted His sovereignty in the very act of creation. He then gave Eve to Adam as a subordinate helper. To both He gave specific instructions. He commanded them to tend the garden, be fruitful, and subdue the whole earth. He also commanded them not to eat of the tree of the knowledge of good and evil. These were the terms of their legal bond recorded in Scripture. The presence of laws implies a legal relation.

---

1. Certainly there is the unseen power of God's Spirit functioning within His creation. Calvin noted in his *Institutes of the Christian Religion*: "For it is the Spirit who, everywhere diffused, sustains all things, causes them to grow, and quickens them in heaven and in earth. Because he is circumscribed by no limits, he is excepted from the category of creatures; but in transfusing into all things his energy, and breathing into them essence, life, and movement, he is indeed plainly divine" (ed. John T. McNeil, trans. F.L. Battles [Philadelphia: Westminster Press, 1960], 1.13.14). Acknowledging this, we are less concerned here with the mystery of how God functions through His creation and more with how He personally relates to it.

God then laid out the consequences for breaking the terms of the agreement. Blessings of the fruit of the earth are implied for obedience but death is the curse for breaking the covenant. These blessings and curses not only applied to Adam but to all his descendants. So from the very beginning we are presented with what it meant for men to "have a relationship" with God. That relationship was one of a covenant. It still is. We could not otherwise hold our doctrine of original sin (Rom. 5:12-21).

The covenant at creation is also sometimes referred to as the Covenant of Works (although this label carries with it other connotations that are not the focus of the present discussion). Even though the word covenant is not explicitly used in the text, the legal structure is obvious. In addition, the prophet Hosea applies the term covenant to Adam's transgression (Hosea 6:7). Perhaps even better is the term Creation Covenant, since it gives due attention to God's word in Jeremiah 33 where He notes a covenant with the created order.

That said, at the very least it is apparent that all of creation is linked to God by a legal bond. We are distinct from God and subordinate to Him as our Creator. Given Adam's headship (which we will discuss in more detail later) we have all broken the terms of the covenant and are therefore deserving of eternal death. If left to our sinful nature, we seek to suppress such truth and thereby seal our place as objects of God's wrath.

> For the wrath of God is revealed from heaven against all ungodliness and unrighteousness of men, who by their unrighteousness suppress the truth. For what can be known about

God is plain to them, because God has shown it to them. For his invisible attributes, namely, his eternal power and divine nature, have been clearly perceived, ever since the creation of the world, in the things that have been made. (Rom. 1:18)

So then, we are left with the uncomfortable but very real position of deserving the curses of that original covenant God made with man. Not only that, all of creation is cursed and in need of redemption. So, what are we to do?

God put together a plan, for His glory and at His good pleasure, to redeem a people to Himself. Think of this in terms of God providing a substitute to take on the consequences for our not keeping the terms of the agreement. How did He do this? He chose to accomplish this once again by relating to His creation through a covenant. Although there are multiple covenant administrations, there is one redemptive covenant. This is commonly called the covenant of grace and is first inaugurated with the promised "seed" in Genesis 3:15. We see this "everlasting" covenant come into view with Abraham.

COVENANT WITH ABRAHAM

God makes a covenant with Abraham and once again we see the covenant structure clearly as the way in which God chooses to relate to mankind. Where the concept of covenant was less "spelled out" at creation, the covenant with Abraham adds to our biblical picture of covenant. In contrast to the covenant made with Adam, this is a covenant with a particular people. The details of this legal agreement between God and Abraham are scattered throughout multiple chapters in Genesis. Again, we are looking for a description of how God relates to mankind generally and here specifically with Abraham.

First, we see God establish Himself as the sovereign. "When Abram was ninety-nine years old the LORD appeared to Abram and said to him, 'I am God Almighty'" (Gen. 17:1). "And He said to him, 'I am the LORD who brought you out from Ur of the Chaldeans to give you this land to possess'" (Gen. 15:7). Is there any mistaking who the sovereign lawgiver is here? God initiates His agreement with Abraham as the one who sets the terms of the agreement.

From there God outlines blessings to Abraham that are both historical and typological. They are realized in part with Abraham and his earthly descendants, but are fully realized among his spiritual descendants.

> And I will make of you a great nation, and I will bless you and make your name great, so that you will be a blessing. (Gen. 12:2) The LORD said to Abram, after Lot had separated from him, "Lift up your eyes and look from the place where you are, northward and southward and eastward and westward, for I will give to you and to your offspring forever." (Gen. 13:14-15)

These promises are found embedded among a series of commands. "Now the LORD said to Abram, 'Go from your country and your kindred and your father's house to the land that I will show you'" (Gen. 12:1). "For I have chosen him, that he may command his children and his household after

WHAT IS A COVENANT?   13

him to keep the way of the LORD by doing righteousness and justice, so that the LORD may bring to Abraham what he has promised him" (Gen. 18:19). Obedience to these commands implies the gifts promised to Abraham. Disobedience necessarily implies the opposite.

God ratifies the bond with Abraham by a peculiar ceremony in Genesis 15. God makes an oath. This oath is one of self-condemnation should He not keep His side of the agreement. To demonstrate such He cuts three animals in half and passes through the pieces. "When the sun had gone down and it was dark, behold, a smoking fire pot and a flaming torch passed between these pieces. On that day the LORD made a covenant with Abram..." (Gen. 15:17–18). Then later in chapter 17 we see God sealing the covenant and giving the sign of circumcision to Abraham and his descendants as an outward display signifying God's intention to fulfill His promise to Abraham.

Although this is a very brief treatment, we can see that God related to Abraham and his descendants through a very real structure—that of an agreement with stipulations, and therefore legal. If all this forensic or judicial talk sounds formal and unloving to you, the truth is that it feels very different depending on your frame of reference. God did in fact save a peculiar people out of Egypt. Prior to that, He made a very exclusive promise to Abraham. The reality is that God can do as He pleases, and we are left with what His Word reveals about Himself.[2]

2. We should not take the emphasis on the legal aspect of the relationship as somehow diminishing the covenant as personal. The relationship is between persons and is therefore personal. It exists between the persons of the Trinity and persons in history. Beyond this it necessarily links these persons in cove-

God gives us our very breath. He makes the sun to shine on the righteous as well as the unrighteous. We are all beneficiaries of God's common grace. That said, He chose to relate uniquely to His elect through the blessing of Jesus Christ.

No man can behave autonomously (on his own will and power, absent of a higher authority). God is sovereign. Through His sovereignty He chose to provide instructions to how we should live our lives. The very presence of these instructions presupposes a legal arrangement between God and His creation. To imagine differently would be to imagine something that was not Christianity at all. With that understood, let's turn to the agreement made between God and the people of Israel.

COVENANT WITH ISRAEL

We have seen how God related through a covenant with Adam at creation and how God's dealing with mankind is further elucidated with the covenant made with Abraham. Keeping in mind the plan of redemption following the Fall detailed above, we now turn to another major covenant administration depicted in Scripture. This one is with Israel, descendants of Abraham who became enslaved to the people of Egypt (a people who did not acknowledge God as Lord and Creator of all things). As the book of Exodus opens, we see God remembering the covenant made with Abraham and his descendants:

---

nant so that they interact in relationship to one another. This relating brings all-encompassing life within the legal bonds. This covenant relationship can be teeming with life through the ministry of the Word, sacraments, prayer, and other facets of the bond.

During those many days the king of Egypt died, and the people of Israel groaned because of their slavery and cried out for help. Their cry for rescue from slavery came up to God. And God heard their groaning, and God remembered his covenant with Abraham, with Isaac, and with Jacob. God saw the people of Israel—and God knew. (Exod. 2:23-25)

A few chapters later we see God relating to the people of Israel again through the covenant structure.

God spoke to Moses and said to him, "I am the LORD. I appeared to Abraham, to Isaac, and to Jacob, as God Almighty, but by my name the LORD I did not make myself known to them. I also established my covenant with them to give them the land of Canaan, the land in which they lived as sojourners. Moreover, I have heard the groaning of the people of Israel whom the Egyptians hold as slaves, and I have remembered my covenant. Say therefore to the people of Israel, 'I am the LORD, and I will bring you out from under the burdens of the Egyptians, and I will deliver you from slavery to them, and I will redeem you with an outstretched arm and with great acts of judgment. I will take you to be my people, and I will be your God, and you shall know that I am the LORD your God, who has brought you out from under the burdens of the Egyptians. I will bring you into the land that I swore to give to Abraham, to Isaac, and to Jacob. I will give it to you for a possession. I am the LORD.'" (Exod. 6:2-8)

Israel was already God's covenant people. They were bound to Him legally. He also, out of His grace, saved them from Egypt, though they did not deserve it. He reminds them of this fact and then proceeds to renew His covenant with them at Sinai.

> ... while Moses went up to God. The LORD called to him out of the mountain, saying, "Thus you shall say to the house of Jacob, and tell the people of Israel: You yourselves have seen what I did to the Egyptians, and how I bore you on eagles' wings and brought you to myself. Now therefore, if you will indeed obey my voice and keep my covenant, you shall be my treasured possession among all peoples, for all the earth is mine; and you shall be to me a kingdom of priests and a holy nation. These are the words that you shall speak to the people of Israel."
>
> So Moses came and called the elders of the people and set before them all these words that the LORD had commanded him. All the people answered together and said, "All that the LORD has spoken we will do." And Moses reported the words of the people to the LORD. (Exod. 19:3-8)

Following this we see the myriad of stipulations laid down for Israel in Exodus and Leviticus. In Deuteronomy we see the renewal of the covenant again with the new generation following the death of the disobedient generation in the wilderness. God acted in judgment toward His people Israel. He executed this judgment according to the terms laid out in the covenant. The same covenant is executed by the following generation. The book of Deuteronomy reads as a legal document between a master and his subjects. God establishes His sovereignty and provides the terms of the covenant along with sanctions for obedience and disobedience. What then became of this people in covenant with God? For a concise picture we turn to Ezekiel 16.

Thus says the LORD GOD to Jerusalem: Your origin and your birth are of the land of the Canaanites; your father was an Amorite and your mother a Hittite. And as for your birth, on the day you were born your cord was not cut, nor were you washed with water to cleanse you...but you were cast out on the open field, for you were abhorred, on the day that you were born.

"And when I passed by you and saw you wallowing in your blood, I said to you in your blood, 'Live!' I said to you in your blood, 'Live!' I made you flourish like a plant of the field...

"When I passed by you again and saw you, behold, you were at the age for love, and I spread the corner of my garment over you and covered your nakedness; I made my vow to you and entered into a covenant with you, declares the Lord GOD, and you became mine.... You grew exceedingly beautiful and advanced to royalty. And your renown went forth among the nations because of your beauty, for it was perfect through the splendor that I had bestowed on you, declares the Lord GOD.

"But you trusted in your beauty and played the whore because of your renown and lavished your whorings on any passerby; your beauty became his. You took some of your garments and made for yourself colorful shrines, and on them played the whore. The like has never been, nor ever shall be. You also took your beautiful jewels of my gold and of my silver, which I

had given you, and made for yourself images of men, and with
them played the whore.... Also my bread that I gave you—I fed
you with fine flour and oil and honey—you set before them
for a pleasing aroma; and so it was, declares the Lord GOD.
And you took your sons and your daughters, whom you had
borne to me, and these you sacrificed to them to be devoured.
Were your whorings so small a matter that you slaughtered my
children and delivered them up as an offering by fire to them?
And in all your abominations and your whorings you did not
remember the days of your youth, when you were naked and
bare, wallowing in your blood. (Ezek. 16:1-22)

God pictures His covenant relation to Israel as a covenant of marriage. His bride was chronically adulterous and
throughout the balance of the Old Testament we see God
bearing with His bride while at the same time sending prophet after prophet to prosecute Israel for her disobedience to
the covenant stipulations. Finally, in the New Testament we
see a new day dawn with the promised seed being shown as a
descendant of Abraham and coming to "save his people from
their sins" (Matt. 1:21).[3]

With the birth of Jesus, the legal bond with Israel again
comes into full view. The Gospels comprise a story of the Son
of God as He makes His way to the cross. During that time
God's bride (Israel) is continually warned and pleaded with

3. The covenant made with David is not treated in this discussion but is important and another expression of the same covenant that weaves through all
of Scripture. Christ is referred to as the Son of David. God promises to raise up
Christ as David's offspring and to establish His kingdom.

to turn to Jesus Christ as the prophesied Christ and promised seed (Gen. 3:15). It begins with John the Baptist coming as the prophesied prophet preaching repentance to God's stubborn bride. Throughout the Gospels there are altercations between Jesus and the Jewish leaders for their unwillingness to recognize and submit to the true gospel. They challenged His authority directly as we see in the book of Matthew. "And when he entered the temple, the chief priests and the elders of the people came up to him as he was teaching, and said, 'By what authority are you doing these things, and who gave you this authority?'" (Matt. 21:23). Jesus follows with His parable of the tenants, aimed directly at Israel.

"Hear another parable. There was a master of a house who planted a vineyard and put a fence around it and dug a winepress in it and built a tower and leased it to tenants, and went into another country. When the season for fruit drew near, he sent his servants to the tenants to get his fruit. And the tenants took his servants and beat one, killed another, and stoned another. Again he sent other servants, more than the first. And they did the same to them. Finally he sent his son to them, saying, 'They will respect my son.' But when the tenants saw the son, they said to themselves, 'This is the heir. Come, let us kill him and have his inheritance.' And they took him and threw him out of the vineyard and killed him. When therefore the owner of the vineyard comes, what will he do to those tenants?" They said to him, "He will put those wretches to a miserable death and let out the vineyard to other tenants who will give him the fruits in their seasons."

Jesus said to them, "Have you never read in the Scriptures: "'The stone that the builders rejected has become the cornerstone; this was the Lord's doing, and it is marvelous in our eyes'?

"Therefore I tell you, the kingdom of God will be taken away from you and given to a people producing its fruits. And the one who falls on this stone will be broken to pieces; and when it falls on anyone, it will crush him."

When the chief priests and the Pharisees heard his parables, they perceived that he was speaking about them. (Matt. 21:33-45)

In Matthew 23, we see the pronouncement of seven woes on the Jewish leaders (as they hold greater responsibility as Israel's authority) and Jesus' lament over the coming destruction of His bride. Chapter 24 details the destruction of the temple in greater detail, and chapter 26 shows the high priest of Israel, Caiaphas, and Jesus confessing that He is the Son of God. He prophesies that Caiaphas will from then on "see the Son of Man seated at the right hand of Power and coming on the clouds of heaven" (v. 64). For the Jewish leaders, who understood Old Testament language, this could refer to none other than the judgment due Israel for breaking the terms of the covenant that bound her to God.

The story of God's covenant relationship with Israel continues as the book of Acts opens with Jesus' ascension and the prophesied outpouring of the Holy Spirit. Directly following this outpouring, Peter speaks to the "Men of Judea and all who dwell in Jerusalem" (Acts 2:14). He quotes the prophet Joel and calls for the people to recognize the Messiah who has come. Many turn to Jesus, and the subsequent story of the early Church accelerates.

Up through the book of Revelation we see a series of Holy Spirit-inspired epistles that guide, encourage, and confront the early church as the confessional body that recognizes Jesus as Messiah and obeys Him. Paul goes to great lengths in his letters to correct early errors brought about by Jewish zealots who claimed Jesus alone was not enough for salvation. He describes Israel as possessing the covenants, law, temple, and promises. It is true that to the collective covenant people Israel belong the "covenants" and "promises," but not every individual in Israel received the promised blessings.

At this point it is very important to remember our earlier discussions. Israel was generally and objectively in covenant with God. They were under the terms of the covenant made with God during the time of Abraham. They were legally bound in a covenant (pictured by God as a marriage covenant) that stipulated blessings for obedience and curses for disobedience. They were obstinately disobedient, and not only had they broken God's moral law, but they had also rejected the very fulfillment of all of the laws that pointed to Jesus as the Christ. They were in grave danger of receiving the punishments stipulated in their covenant with the Creator God.

In Romans 11, Paul describes a vine from which Israel is pruned and Gentiles grafted in. The root of this vine is Jesus (Is. 11:10). In the book of Revelation, we witness something that has been continually misinterpreted during this era where dispensationalism has held such a foothold in evangelical culture. We witness the legal divorce of the bride of Israel for her sins of spiritual adultery and murder (Matt. 21:33–44; 23:29–35; Acts 7:51–53; Rev. 18:24). She is executed with the destruction of the temple in AD 70. This was the consequence of disobedience spelled out in the covenant made between God and His people Israel. We then see a beautiful picture of God's new bride, the church, being carried over the threshold into the new heavens and new earth as a spotless bride. This church is none other than the true descendants of Abraham, the elect of God made up of believing Jews and Gentiles.

But what of the church here on earth? The eschatological church is indeed a true bride, but what of the bride of Christ on earth here and now? How is this church seen or perceived in space and time? Certainly the hearts of the elect are beyond our perception. To answer this question we must turn back to the covenant. As we have stated, God relates to people on earth through the structure of a covenant. This very structure governs the new bride of Christ, the church.

THE NEW COVENANT[4]

In Matthew 16 we see the first mention of this new bride we call the church. Jesus says that He will build His church upon the confession of Peter. What was Peter's confession? It was

4. Throughout this book, "church" will most often refer to the New Testament church versus the general called-out "assembly" or "congregation" of both the Old and New Testaments.

that Jesus was "the Christ, the Son of the living God" (Matt. 16:16). Jesus then goes on to say that the church will see final victory and that it will be linked to heaven. "I will give you the keys of the kingdom, and whatever you bind on earth shall be bound in heaven, and whatever you loose on earth shall be loosed in heaven" (Matt. 16:19). How is it linked to heaven? To put it another way, how will the church on earth be sensibly determined and how will it objectively relate to a supernatural God? You guessed it—it will be through the covenant.

Those that comprise the New Testament community are those who confessionally place themselves under the terms of the covenant. In the New Testament we see no altering of the structure and form of God's covenant bride. God still relates to people on earth, in time and in space. God chooses to reveal Himself and work out His redemptive history through a people in an objective covenant with Him. The decree of election before the foundation of the world and His elect are not visible to us, but the covenant relationship is visible. The visible display of placing oneself under the terms of the covenant is baptism. We will deal more with this initiatory rite and the terms of the covenant in the next chapter; for now, suffice it to say that there is a New Covenant bride on earth in history.

All men are in covenant relation to God, as discussed earlier, but there is a special community of "called-out" ones through whom God intends to accomplish the redemption of creation. He is their God and they have commands by which to live and conduct themselves as God's people. There are corresponding blessings and curses associated within the terms of the covenant. Again, this is how God has chosen to relate to mankind. We have no other biblical model.

There are surely certain differences in the New Covenant administration, such as the gift of the Holy Spirit and the full, written revelation of the Word of God, but these changes do not necessitate a change in structure of God's relation to His bride. These are primarily differences in power and revelation, not structure.

ALL OF SCRIPTURE AS COVENANT

Until now we have shown how God relates to mankind through specific covenantal administrations throughout history.[5] God has always related through a legal bond with His creation. The supernatural manifests itself in the natural through a set of terms presented by the Creator. Not until the New Covenant administration was this covenant so completely available as God's Word in written form. God gave us His Word in Scripture. His Word is final. His written revelation is now closed. Interestingly, what we will find is that the whole of Scripture is in the form of a covenant. It is incredibly significant but not surprising that God's only revealed Word to us is in the very form of a legal document.

Meredith Kline, in his landmark book *The Structure of Biblical Authority*, builds on the work of George Mendenhall by discovering the form of suzerainty treaties of the ancient

5. Since we are primarily concerned with God's relating to mankind, we will not cover the issue of the Trinity in covenant. That said, let me acknowledge that relationship as fundamental to God relating to His people and their relationships with one another.

Near East and their close similarities to the form of Scripture. He makes the bold statement, "It will emerge, we believe, that for purposes of reappraising the Old Testament canon, the most significant development in the last quarter-century has not been the Dead Sea scroll finds but discoveries made concerning the covenants of the Old Testament in light of ancient Near Eastern treaty diplomacy."[6] In short, these ancient treaties detail the events following a successful military campaign wherein the victorious king draws up a treaty detailing the terms of peace. Cornelis van der Waal provides a concise description of such treaties:

> Political treaties have been discovered that were made between kings of equal standing, for instance, those of Egypt and of the Hittite empire (parity covenants). Even more tests have been found which refer to a treaty between a great king and the subjected king of a conquered country, a vassal state or protectorate (suzerainty covenants).
>
> In the course of time, the treaty texts have undergone amendments. Obviously, fashion is not confined to clothing alone. The sequence of the various parts may change and other parts may have been omitted or described less clearly. It appears, however, that even before Abraham's time there was standardized covenant terminology.

---

6. Meredith G. Kline, *The Structure of Biblical Authority*, 2nd ed. (Eugene, OR: Wipf & Stock, 1997), 25.

According to a rather general consensus (no small thing in the scientific world!), the ideal structure of such a dynastic treaty would look like this:

I   Preamble

II   Historical Prologue

III   Stipulations

IV   Curses and Blessings

V   Invocation of Witnesses

VI   Directions for Disposition and Public Reading[7]

Now keeping in mind van der Waal's statement that "Archaeology is the handmaid of biblical interpretation—not its master,"[8] it should be no surprise to us, given the previous discussion, that the Bible itself is laid out in the form of these ancient treaties. God is in fact our suzerain; we are His vassals. We operate and relate to Him under these terms. Kline goes on in his book to show that the very founding of Scripture "coincided with the formal founding of Israel as the kingdom of God."[9] He then demonstrates that the whole of the Old Testament is in covenant form and represents the covenant with Israel, the people of God. He does not stop there but goes on to describe the structure of the New Testament:

> In the case of the New Testament as in that of the Old Testament, acceptance of its own claims as to its primary divine

7. Cornelis van der Waal, *The Covenantal Gospel* (Neerlandia, Alberta: Inheritance Publications, 1990), 19.

8. Van der Waal, 19.

9. Meredith G. Kline, *The Structure of Biblical Authority*, 38.

authorship leads to recognition of its pervasively covenantal nature and purpose. For the New Testament so received will be understood as the word of the ascended Lord of the new covenant, by which he structures the community of the new covenant and orders the faith and life of his servant people in their consecrated relationship to him. And then the human authors of the New Testament books, authorized by their Lord to speak his word, will be seen to function as his "ministers of the new covenant" (cf. 2 Cor. 3:6). With respect to immediate as well as ultimate provenance, the *Sitz im Leben* of the New Testament books is fundamentally covenantal. They all arise out of a covenantal source of authority and all address themselves to the covenant community.[10]

Given that the very founding of Scripture coincided with the founding of the kingdom of Israel, we should not be at all surprised to see the canon (or covenant document) coinciding with the covenantal divorce of that kingdom and the taking of the bride of Christ in covenant as the founding of the archetypical kingdom of God that will extend throughout all of the earth and on into eternity.

COVENANT STRUCTURE REVISITED

Given this understanding, our discussion regarding structure would not be complete without visiting further the structure of the covenant we see in Scripture. I have spoken to this above in relation to the similar structure of the ancient treaties, but

---

10. Kline, *The Structure of Biblical Authority*, 71.

we must return to the beginning of our discussion where we were looking at the covenantal form given to us by Scripture itself. This structure will have direct bearing on subsequent chapters and is vitally important.

In addition to Kline, there is another writer whose contribution to understanding the covenant is significant: Ray Sutton and his book *That You May Prosper*. He begins with a short history of covenant thinking and then goes on to detail and defend the clearest picture of what comprises the elements of the biblical covenant. Over and against what the secular world identified as the key component of the ancient treaties, Sutton identifies five components or key concepts of the covenant in the Word of God. Not only are they identified, but he goes on to show how the Bible in its structure displays each of them. The five components are transcendence, hierarchy, ethics, sanctions, and continuity provisions.

1. *Transcendence* is what was noted above beginning with Adam at creation. Within a divine covenant agreement there is an establishment of God as the supreme sovereign, transcendent over and distinct from His creation. He alone has the power over all. Man is not sovereign. He is subject to the will of his Creator. As one might expect, establishing who has authority in the legal relationship is a given.

2. *Hierarchy* is the component of the agreement that spells out who has the authority to act on the authority given by God. God acts through mankind and gives man a corporate

reporting structure through which He takes that action. This is functional subordination.

3. *Ethics* are merely the rules or laws that govern the relationship between the parties. As mentioned, God establishes His authority, establishes Himself as Creator, and is the only party that possesses the power to command or set the stipulations of the agreement. These are provided to us in His inspired Word.

4. *Sanctions* are those consequences that follow from either keeping (positive) or breaking the laws (negative) governing our bond with God. An oath is taken that binds us and formally sets us under the terms of the agreement.

5. *Continuity provisions* are set forth to give direction to the covenant relationship for future generations. These provisions outline the extension of authority and rule into the future.[11]

Whether or not there are other distinct facets of ancient Near Eastern treaties of that time, these are the characteristics that keep surfacing as the core of the covenant structure we see in God's Word. These are consistent with the very foundational tenants of our Christian doctrine. We acknowledge God as sovereign. We carry out His will here on earth. He gives us His Word by which to live. He blesses and punishes in time and in eternity. The concept of eternity, of heaven and hell, are the continuity provisions laid out in Scripture. God made provision for His people to inherit eternal life. Those that do

---

11. Ray Sutton, *That You May Prosper: Dominion by Covenant* (Tyler, TX: Institute for Christian Economics, 1987), 6–7.

not believe in Him come under His eternal judgment. This is Christian doctrine at its core.

So, we return to where we began with regard to our "relationship with God." No longer does the oft-heard phrase have to be a vague reference to our warm feelings toward God, the amount of prayers we pray, or obedience to any number of behaviors labeled as Christ-like. A "good" relationship with God is living life obediently and joyously under the terms of the legal bond we have with Him as our Creator and King. The covenant document is none other than the inspired and written Word of God, the Bible. It represents God as our sovereign and provides a representative hierarchy through which to be governed according to the commands laid out in the entirety of Scripture. The document includes not only the commands but also the blessings and curses that follow from either keeping or breaking the terms of the covenant. And as mentioned above, the covenant document leaves us with the provisions of future inheritance for those keeping the terms and future disinheritance for those who break the terms of the divine agreement.

If this legal structure seems like a harsh and unloving "legalism," we must remind ourselves that those who keep the covenant cannot do so on their own. The topic of God's working and our responsibility is not within the scope of this book, but there has been much written on the subject that is helpful. For our purposes, Paul's words in Romans will have to suffice. "You will say to me then, 'Why does he still find fault? For who can resist his will?' But who are you, O man, to answer back to God? Will what is molded say to its molder, 'Why have you made me like this?'" (Rom. 9:19-20).

God sets forth the terms through which we are to relate to Him and He to us. We are to be responsible men and are to remain thankful to God for any of our ability to respond in obedience. It is Jesus Christ who was the sacrifice for sins and through the Holy Spirit will give power to persevere to all those He has called according to His purpose and good pleasure.

With this in mind, we need to go further in our investigation of the covenant concept. I have stated that the covenant is the structure through which God has chosen to relate to His creation. That said, what is unique about a covenant from a biblical standpoint? Is it just a peace treaty? Are not all contracts with terms and stipulations covenants? This is the subject that we will cover in the next chapter.

CHAPTER TWO:
THREE COVENANT INSTITUTIONS IN HISTORY

IN CHAPTER 1, I SOUGHT TO HIGHLIGHT how we connect or relate to God. The supernatural or unseen must interact somehow with the natural and material.[1] If we presuppose that God is distinct from us and over us, yet ever-present and intimately involved with us, then there must be a way through which God relates to His creation. Many mystical religions see God as a part of or connected to man or nature. In this way men and women relate to Him as a part

---

1. For those who think this feels a bit Aristotelian, it is not meant to be so. I am merely distinguishing the seen from the unseen. In biblical terms, there is heaven and earth. There is an infinite God who rules over finite men. "He said to them, 'You are from below; I am from above. You are of this world; I am not of this world'" (John 8:23). Some may prefer the terms historical and eschatological.

of themselves (i.e., not distinct). Those that deny God seek no relation at all.

So, how does the Christian view this relation with God? As we have now seen, we relate to God in time and space through a legal bond with Him. This legal bond shows His sovereignty over us, the structure of His sovereignty on earth, the laws we are to live by, the consequences of obedience and disobedience, and what happens to the bond upon our death.

That said, other legal agreements can have this same structure, so what makes the biblical covenant wholly unique? The unique identifier is that it acknowledges God in a legal context as the supreme authority to declare what is right and wrong along with the associated judgments. It acknowledges the higher authority of our Creator, the God of the Bible, as over and above any authority within His creation.

So we are left with the question, if there is a covenant in place between us and our God, how does He execute judgments of blessings and curses on earth? First, He certainly works through all of His created order to execute consequences of blessing and curses. There exists cause and effect according to the order He established. If you jump out of a tall building, you will be hurt. If you continually lie, you will not be trusted. If you do not cultivate your fields, you will grow hungry. If you cultivate your garden and God sends you rain, then you will eat. God's Word speaks to all of life, and it is where we derive our ethical standard for everything.

That said, did God just leave us to live under His rule directly, experiencing the response of God's creation when we obey or disobey with perhaps a miracle for good behavior and the occasional lightning bolt for disobedience? The answer in part is what we have already discussed in chapter 1. God does not work through creation mystically. He works through His creation representatively. He chooses to use men to carry out His rule on earth.

This should make sense to us. A visible God that we can touch does not directly govern the affairs of men. He has always chosen men to do this. These men are answerable to God and act in His authority and within His established hierarchy to bring about His rule on earth. So can all men claim they have this possession of God's authority and judge accordingly? How does all of this work?

Again, we must turn to the covenant document, the Bible, for our answers. In it, we see three institutional hierarchies that legitimately claim this authority. These institutional hierarchies are covenantally bound. The structure of a covenant institution is the same or could ideally be the same as the structure of any governed institution. The defining point is the authority to execute God's judgment. A covenant institution is an oath-bound institution through which God has chosen to execute His judgments in history. The ability to call down and carry out God's judgment and sanctions (blessings and curses) is what makes an institution covenantal. The only examples given in the Bible that have such authority to invoke God's judgments are the family, church, and state (civil government). All answer to God Himself. They are bound in a legal bond or covenant that is ratified in an oath to Him.

Think about it this way: the Bible is the covenant document. In it, we see outlined how stipulated judgments are carried out. It gives a structure through which God's rule is to be carried out on earth. Predictably it is a covenant structure. All three institutions (governments) are defined with boundaries and are central to carrying out God's will on earth.

REPRESENTATION

Before we speak in greater detail about the specific institutions mentioned above, we need to be sure we are clear on this idea of man representing God's authority on earth. There are men on earth who represent God and His will. They quite literally make decisions and judgments according to that will (as laid out in His Word, or covenant). They express the will of God on earth. God acts on earth. He acts through men. One of the best summations of this idea is found in an excerpt by Gary North within a discussion on obedience to covenant law:

> Man thinks that he is disobeying God on his own account, in his own authority, but in fact, man must serve only one master. Ethically, he subordinates himself to Satan when he refuses to obey God. He comes under the hierarchical rule of another master. Man may think he is acting autonomously, but he in fact is simply shifting masters. God or Baal? This was Elijah's question (1 Kings 18:21). God or mammon? This was Jesus' question (Matt. 6:24).
>
> But neither God nor Satan normally appears to an individual. Each sends human representatives. Men represent God

in positions of corporate responsibility. God has established three monopolistic institutions: church, State, and family. The head of each can serve God or Satan, and those under him are sanctified (set apart) institutionally.

Soldiers live or die in terms of decisions made by their superiors. Nations rise and fall in terms of the decisions of their national leaders. An individual's success or failure in history cannot be discussed without reference to the institutional hierarchies above and below him, and their success or failure.[2]

This is seemingly very simple to understand, but for some reason we do not commonly acknowledge this in how we conduct our affairs on earth. To the extent that we understand this concept and how it is manifested within God-ordained structures is the extent to which we will corporately extend the rule of God on earth through human hearts. The importance of grasping this is expressed in the very words of Jesus as He taught us to pray, "Your kingdom come, your will be done, on earth as it is in heaven" (Matt. 6:10).

BIBLICAL OATHS

So, how then do men legally bind themselves to God and then act in positions of authority? What does this look like? How did we come to identify family, church, and state? The answer lies in the biblical perspective on oaths.

---

2. Gary North, *Tools of Dominion: The Case Laws of Exodus* (Tyler, TX: Institute for Christian Economics, 1990), 78.

We see from Scripture that oaths were a legal device that consisted of making a pledge or statement of fact obliging the oath-taker to fulfill the vow or pledge, or represent truth. An oath appealed to God as ultimate witness and judge should the oath-taker keep or break the vow, represent or misrepresent truth. Hebrews 6:16 tells us, "For people swear by something greater than themselves, and in all their disputes an oath is final for confirmation."

When looking at biblical examples of oaths, it is clear that these oaths legally bind to the Lord. What does it mean to "bind"? The oath-taker is now liable to receive blessings or punishments as stipulated by the agreement bound by the oath. An oath that binds a covenant is very literally calling on God to punish or bless according to the stipulations of that covenant. For the one taking the oath, it is self-condemning should the terms be broken; it is calling for blessing should they not.

The central point is that an oath invokes or calls down God's blessings or curses. These must be enforceable. Now we are back to the earlier discussion. Who carries these out? Is it some miracle reward or a lightning bolt from the sky? Not at all. God works through man.

More than that, we see God choosing to give authority in separate jurisdictions. These jurisdictions have their unique authority and unique sanctions. God outlines the boundaries of those jurisdictions, provides their laws, and outlines the extent of the sanctions (or binding forces) they may carry out. Put simply, God's authority is worked out through people individually, but also bound together as institutions representing

Him in their God-delegated sphere on earth. By their oath, they put themselves under the authority of the institution and therefore under God's ordained authority on earth. Those ordained to represent God in those institutions are commanded to lead and hold accountable the members according to the love, character, and law of God.

How do we identify these institutions? God identifies them by showing that each is set up under oath, possessing His authority, and that they are the only institutions in the Word of God identified as such. The authoritative oath, or oath binding to God's authoritative institutions, is the defining difference between these covenantal institutions and institutions bound by contract. These are the family, church, and state. They are the only examples in Scripture of institutions that are given God's authority to carry out the binding force of sanctions. Therefore, we are to use God's revealed pattern or structure to carry out His authority. These are the institutions through which we would expect God to expand His kingdom on earth.

THE FAMILY

The first covenantal institution is the family. Where does the family begin and how do we know that it is an institution bound by covenantal oath, representing God's authority and carrying out His rule on earth? To answer this we need to look at Scripture to find where and how the family unit is established, the scope of its authority, jurisdictional limits, and sanctions as well as how it continues through time here on earth and into eternity.

THE FAMILY ESTABLISHED

As we all might expect, we see the family first established in Genesis with Adam and Eve.

> And the rib that the LORD God had taken from the man he made into a woman and brought her to the man. Then the man said,
> "This at last is bone of my bones and flesh of my flesh;
> she shall be called Woman, because she was taken out of Man."
> Therefore a man shall leave his father and his mother and hold fast to his wife, and they shall become one flesh. (Gen. 2:22–24)

From the inception of the family we see two things. One, there is headship; God established His hierarchy from the outset. To Adam He gave authority and responsibility to represent Him. In addition, God states that as generations progress, the children will break from their family heads and be bound as one flesh together. Leaving (`azab) is the same Hebrew word used for the apostasy of God's people from the covenant and so pictures the end of a covenant bond.[3] How else can we be sure that this is a covenantal relationship? Where is the lawful oath that binds them together? The answer is found first in

---

3. Ray Sutton, *That You May Prosper*, 143.

how God refers to the institution of marriage and also what the Bible has to say about vows.

Scripture is very clear on the definition of marriage. Marriage is not just a bringing together physically or contractually. We know this because God frequently makes reference to His marriage to His people throughout Scripture. Of His people Israel He says, "I made my vow to you and entered into a covenant with you, declares the Lord GOD, and you became mine" (Ezek. 16:8). There was no contract and certainly no physical union that took place. When God married His people, He entered into a covenant relationship with them. He was establishing Himself as their God. He declared Himself head in keeping with the headship assigned to Adam in Genesis. He also gave His laws that carried blessings for obedience and curses for disobedience. And finally, He outlined the inheritance or disinheritance of His bride.

Marriage is an oath-bound covenant. "For thus says the Lord GOD: I will deal with you as you have done, you who have despised the oath in breaking the covenant" (Ezek. 16:59). God describes it most clearly in the book of Malachi: "The LORD was witness between you and the wife of your youth, to whom you have been faithless, though she is your companion and your wife by covenant" (2:14).

So following Adam and Eve, what does the establishment of marriage look like between a man and a woman? Predictably, in the West we see marriages established according to the pattern of Scripture. Vows before God are taken to establish a legal bond. These vows are sanctioned by Scripture. Numbers

30:2 says that "if a man vows a vow to the LORD, or swears an oath to bind himself by a pledge, he shall not break his word. He shall do according to all that proceeds out of his mouth."

The full chapter in Numbers outlines for us that vows can legitimately be made under God's authority and that they carry the full weight of a self-condemning oath. Marriages are to be established just as described in Scripture. They come into being with the presence of legally enforceable vows. The "leave and cleave" of Genesis 2 shows us this. God's relationship to His people pictures it. Even in the New Testament we see a direct comparison of the marriage between a man and a woman to the covenant relationship between Jesus Christ and the church (Eph. 5:22–33).

HOUSEHOLD AUTHORITY

Knowing that marriage is a biblical institution established through a covenant, what does its authority look like and over what jurisdiction or areas of life does it exercise that authority? First, the family is a governed unit that God has called to be fruitful and multiply over the earth. Quite literally, the family is to display the character of God and work out that character in everything it does.

Why was the family instituted in the first place? The Bible says that Eve was given to Adam as a "help meet" (made suitable) in tending the garden. The family exists to glorify God together through their work and in doing so, subdue the earth. To carry this out, the family, however small or large, must be governed.

As we now know, God's authority is extended through man in the form of a legal bond. As such, God designates a family hierarchy through which to work. He has chosen the man to be the covenant head. Though at times this authority may be exploited, the biblical intent is that the man is to rule, not as a tyrant, but in love over his household as Christ Himself would (Eph. 5). The man's headship as well as the family's calling to subdue the earth is the same in the Old and New Testaments. "For the man is not of the woman; but the woman of the man. Neither was the man created for the woman; but the woman for the man" (1 Cor. 11:8–9, KJV). "Likewise, wives, be subject to your own husbands" (1 Pet. 3:1). The hierarchy of authority extends down to the children:

> Children, obey your parents in the Lord, for this is right.
> "Honor your father and mother" (this is the first command-
> ment with a promise), "that it may go well with you and that
> you may live long in the land." Fathers, do not provoke your
> children to anger, but bring them up in the discipline and in-
> struction of the Lord. (Eph. 6:1–4)

The jurisdiction even extends to the servants within the house-hold: "Slaves, obey your masters with fear and trembling, with a sincere heart, as you would Christ" (Eph. 6:5).

We can clearly see that the family is a unit, bound by cov-enant and ruled by the law of God through His established hierarchy. It follows, then, that God delegates the teaching of the law of God to the family as well as the carrying out of sanctions through the offices discussed above. Again, if the family is one of God's ordained institutions to carry out His authority, we must see the presence of a covenant oath as well as the ability to carry out positive and negative sanctions according to established ethics.

What does this look like in the family? We saw in Ephesians God's prescription to bring up children in the discipline and admonition of the Lord. But we see such commands throughout the Scriptures—for example, in Deuteronomy 6:6-9: "And these words that I command you today shall be on your heart. You shall teach them diligently to your children, and shall talk of them when you sit in your house, and when you walk by the way, and when you lie down, and when you rise." If the laws of our home are to be the laws of God, what happens when our children keep them? They are then blessed by rewards. What if they break them? Parents bring about consequences. This includes the use of the rod (Prov. 13:24; 22:15; 23:13; 29:15).

God's authority is carried out through His established hierarchy within His prescribed jurisdiction that extends to anyone within the household. That authority is carried out according to His character and enforced through parents by the use of biblically prescribed consequences for obedience and disobedience.

FAMILY SUCCESSION

In keeping with our understanding of the family as a covenant institution, there must be terms that speak to succession should there be divorce (lawful or unlawful) or death. Let's get the last one out of the way first. There is no extension of the covenant family after death. There are certainly provisions of the family unit on earth in the event of the death of one or more parties, but there is no continuation of the covenant bond into eternity. Jesus makes this clear in His response to the Sadducees: "But Jesus answered them, 'You are wrong, because you know neither the Scriptures nor the power of God. For in the resurrection they neither marry nor are given in marriage, but are like angels in heaven'" (Matt. 22:30).

As to terminated covenants here on earth, God does make provision for divorce. The covenant agreement may be terminated lawfully on the grounds of adultery. This is not required, but it is lawful: "But I say to you that everyone who divorces his wife, except on the ground of sexual immorality, makes her commit adultery, and whoever marries a divorced woman commits adultery" (Matt. 5:32).[4]

Perhaps the more important aspect of the succession of the family covenant is that it is through family bonds that wealth is transferred. I am not speaking only about money and physical assets. The love of God, wisdom, and the understanding of Scripture are the most important aspects of family inheritance. It takes all of these as well as physical assets to carry out the family's God-given purpose. The family carries out this purpose through procreation, evangelism, charity, productive work, and other biblically prescribed methods for

---

4. There may be other biblically lawful grounds for the termination of a marriage covenant. This would involve a discussion of other capital offenses in general from a scriptural standpoint, and such a discussion lies outside the scope of this book.

subduing the earth. It does this with God's authority within the terms of a covenant.

THE STATE

Since much of the rest of this book is dedicated to an understanding of the church covenant, we will save the discussion of that institution until the end of this chapter. For now, I will briefly touch on the idea of a biblical civil covenant often designated as the state. First, we need to rid ourselves of some very common misconceptions.

Some may question whether the state lies within the scope of the Christ's rule on earth. They see the civil realm as neutral territory that is governed by a set of neutral laws common to all men.[5] The resulting understanding is that God extends His rule in the Christian church and Christian family but civil affairs are relatively left alone until the Second Advent.

This was much easier to accept at a time following the Reformation when Jesus' authority was widely recognized in the Western world. The "neutral" ground of the state was moving along pretty well, and with the added insights of the Enlightenment, it seemed as if there was a common law that

---

5. Some would say that it is not neutral law but that it is a natural law common to all men for life outside the church. If it is common to all men, then it is in some sense ethically neutral. Fallen man cannot ascertain such laws outside of the special revelation of God. The pagan "knows" God, to be sure, as is outlined in Romans 1. He does not, though, know God's rule for living life in every area without God's revealed Word in Scripture. The same is true for the believer. The only difference is that the believer's eyes are open to the special revelation through the power of the Holy Spirit.

could sustain that realm without having to wrestle with the idea of applying biblical law to the state.

Those times have changed. As a result of not acknowledging biblical law and Christ's authority in the civil covenant (as well as in the others), we are confronted with a godless civil realm that only has remnants of the structure borrowed from Scripture many years ago. Hence, we have two major reactions to the predicament in which we find ourselves.

One reaction is to label such ground neutral (or in some circles non-redemptive) and pray hard for the Second Coming in hopes of witnessing Jesus' victory in a final showdown with Satan, ushering in the new heaven and new earth. Inconsistently though, those with this reaction still feel obliged to involve themselves in politics to fight major battles, such as abortion. This is because they inherently know what they do not claim. There is no neutral (or common) ground on earth.

The other reaction to the situation has been for God to prick the hearts of many, causing them to reject the claim of a neutral civil realm. Not only are they convinced that God does intend to rule in this area through His revealed Word, they also openly acknowledge the power of the Holy Spirit to bring about such a rule.

Does this line of thinking necessarily lead to a bloody revolution, seeking to overthrow any pagan government and replace it with Christian men bent on enforcing the law of God? Not at all. Why? Because this is not how God has ordained it. How does it happen? Just as we suspect it would: the church evangelizes, the Holy Spirit convicts of sin, and people are converted.

Over time those people seek to set up the rules of their homes to reflect the character of God, and work in their church to do the same. But they do not stop there. They seek to do the same in their communities. They work within the established hierarchies in each area to bring about godly environments.

What do I mean by working through the established hierarchies? An example might be the recently converted mother with an unbelieving husband. She does not go home and kill her husband, or subject him by force so she can then set up her household and teach her children according to the Word of God. No, she begins to pray and influence her home from the inside out. Where there is opportunity, she governs her areas of influence in the home biblically. Over time her husband may come to faith. Through the discipleship of a good church he learns God's Word, and over time he works to apply it to his household. Perhaps before the children are grown you have a household that better pictures Christ's rule.

Why should we expect anything different when it comes to civil rule? God does not sanction outside-in revolution in the state any more than He would in the home.

The purpose of this book is not to debate God's involvement in the civil realm. I am taking for granted that God intends to establish His rule in all areas of life on earth in history. There is one King, Jesus Christ. There is one law revealed in the one source of special revelation that we have and that governs everything. There was one definitive victory at the cross. There is one battle going on to manifest that victory in history. There is only one battlefield. There are two sides. One side has the Holy Spirit's power.

THE STATE ESTABLISHED

We first clearly see the idea of a civil covenant established in the book of Exodus. Following the Exodus from Egypt, we find Moses hearing cases and solving disputes for the people of Israel (Exod. 17:13). God had not yet formally established the Aaronic priesthood, the ark, or the tabernacle. We do, though, see families and community, and we would expect that he was governing these areas. The question is, by what law was he doing this?

He was using the law of God. He was representing God to the people and the people to God. "You shall represent the people before God and bring their cases to God, and you shall warn them about the statutes and the laws, and make them know the way in which they must walk and what they must do" (Exod. 18:19–20). This was representative government. Beyond this we also see God's prescription for an appeals court system:

> Moreover, look for able men from all the people, men who fear God, who are trustworthy and hate a bribe, and place such men over the people as chiefs of thousands, of hundreds, of fifties, and of tens. And let them judge the people at all times. Every great matter they shall bring to you, but any small matter they shall decide themselves. So it will be easier for you, and they will bear the burden with you. (Exod. 18:21–23)

These able men pictured both representation and hierarchy. It is within this context that we find Israel camped before Mount Sinai. They are about to receive the fullest revelation to date of God's character as represented through His law. The laws that were to be given covered every area of life.

> They set out from Rephidim and came into the wilderness of Sinai, and they encamped in the wilderness. There Israel encamped before the mountain, while Moses went up to God. The LORD called to him out of the mountain, saying, "Thus you shall say to the house of Jacob, and tell the people of Israel: You yourselves have seen what I did to the Egyptians, and how I bore you on eagles' wings and brought you to myself. Now therefore, if you will indeed obey my voice and keep my covenant, you shall be my treasured possession among all peoples, for all the earth is mine; and you shall be to me a kingdom of priests and a holy nation. These are the words that you shall speak to the people of Israel."
>
> So Moses came and called the elders of the people and set before them all these words that the LORD had commanded him. All the people answered together and said, "All that the LORD has spoken we will do." And Moses reported the words of the people to the LORD. (Exod. 19:2–8)

We see here Israel being bound to uphold the covenant through the public testimony of the group of elders that represented the entire body. But the laws were just for Israel, you may say. But what about Egypt? Was Pharaoh not to obey his

Creator? It is true that Israel was delivered by God for a special purpose and through their covenant with God they had opportunity for special blessings and were also under the threat of greater curse. But just because Israel was in a covenant bond with God, did that mean it was wrong for them to steal, but it was not wrong for Pharaoh? Did Israel have to obey laws about fair treatment of household servants, but Pharaoh had free reign to oppress his? Evidently not, since God punished him for that very sin and freed Israel.

Were the surrounding peoples not obliged to govern their civilizations according to the rule of their Creator as outlined in Scripture? Were pagan nations free in God's eyes to mistreat the widow and the orphan? Certainly not. Were there really two different laws governing humanity, or just one law, and an opportunity to formally covenant with the one lawgiver? Deuteronomy 4:6-8 makes it clear that Israel's civil law code was to be held out as an example for the nations to follow.

We see in Exodus God establishing a hierarchy and system for governing the civil and priestly realms. They both have laws. They both require hierarchies. They both are subject to representation. Both can be in covenant with God. They are both bound by the public oaths of their representatives. This cannot be written off as not applying to anyone but God's sanctified people living under a "theocracy." Every nation is a theocracy. All nations establish laws. Laws are not amoral. Laws declare a religion of some kind.

In Exodus, God was establishing His law as supreme and displaying His relationship to His people through a special covenant. Pharaoh too was under God's covenant at creation. He did not abide by the terms. He represented his people. His and their firstborn sons were killed. God intends for all men to govern their actions in community according to His law. Just as God holds the pagan accountable to marry and conduct His house by His law; just as He holds them responsible for confessing Christ and placing themselves under the rule of the church; so does He expect the pagan to acknowledge His authority in the civil realm and place himself under His rule and to govern according to God's law through a special covenant bond. Why is there a national covenant in order? Because it provides boundaries, jurisdiction, and a structure for governing people according to the law of God. The only alternative is to create boundaries, jurisdiction, and a rule according to some contrived law of man. Man is fallen. In the end this will not work out any differently from how it did under Pharaoh.

CIVIL AUTHORITY

Although this civil authority was established in the Old Testament, where do we see the civil institution after the coming of Christ, and what is the nature of such civil authority as outlined in Scripture? The most well-known passage answering these questions is in Romans 13:

> Let every person be subject to the governing authorities. For there is no authority except from God, and those that exist have been instituted by God. Therefore whoever resists the authorities resists what God has appointed, and those who

resist will incur judgment. For rulers are not a terror to good conduct, but to bad. Would you have no fear of the one who is in authority? Then do what is good, and you will receive his approval, for he is God's servant for your good. But if you do wrong, be afraid, for he does not bear the sword in vain. For he is the servant of God, an avenger who carries out God's wrath on the wrongdoer. Therefore one must be in subjection, not only to avoid God's wrath but also for the sake of conscience. For because of this you also pay taxes, for the authorities are ministers of God, attending to this very thing. Pay to all what is owed to them: taxes to whom taxes are owed, revenue to whom revenue is owed, respect to whom respect is owed, honor to whom honor is owed. (vv. 1-7)

Here we see that Jesus is King over all authorities, and they are ultimately subject to Him. Paul says that God is the author of all institutions that possess authority. He vested them with their authority. He labels them as servants or ministers in His name. Does this not fit the understanding we have from the previous discussions? God rules. He rules through men. He rules through institutions in covenant with Him. "Civil government always exercises God-given authority as a representative of God (Romans 13:1-7) either explicitly or implicitly. Government is therefore *representative*: it represents God to man, and man to God."[6]

---

6. Gary North, *Healer of the Nations: Biblical Blueprints for International Relations* (Ft. Worth, TX: Dominion Press, 1987), 26, italics in original.

But what of godless civil governments? This does not seem to fit the discussion. In the very context of the verses cited above, Paul is under the jurisdiction of the Roman government—a government that could hardly be characterized as ruling according to the law of God.

We have to ask ourselves some basic questions lest we quickly become confused. "For rulers are not a terror to good conduct, but to bad." What defines good and bad conduct? Scripture.[7]

So, where does the terrible Roman emperor Nero fit in? It seems he was the very antithesis of the rulers characterized by Paul. He seemed to be a terror to good conduct. "For he is the servant of God, an avenger who carries out God's wrath on the wrongdoer." Again, a ruler like Nero would seem to be someone who many times carries out wrath on the "rightdoer." Unless Paul's words are senseless we must conclude that, whereas God sets up and gives authoritative institutions their power, all rulers do not rightly reflect His judgments. Rome as well as any other civil authority was subject to the authority of Christ. They were in fact servants, and there is no mistaking that they have been called upon to serve according to the will

7. Here again I understand there to be those that say nature communicates what defines good and bad conduct as well. It is natural or common law shared by a realm outside of the church. This gives our depraved minds too much credit. Whereas both pagan and Christian surely learn over time to look before crossing a busy street so as to be "preserved" by common grace, neither the pagan nor the Christian can know God's prescribed sanction for the drunk driver who swerves and kills that careful pagan or Christian pedestrian. The pagan civil servant cannot in his blind state know how to represent the rule of God and execute His judgments in specific situations. He needs the assistance of Scripture.

of God. "Serve the Lord with fear, and rejoice with trembling" (Ps. 2:11). The ruler must act with Scripture as his standard. He is a civil minister. If he does not, his rule will eventually be cut short, and he, like all, will face the final judgment, as Nero did.

Why would Paul include this passage if it were not describing the Roman government that was ruling over the church in Rome? James Willson, in his exposition of Romans 13:1-7, provides the following three reasons, among others:

> [I]t was designed to show that civil government is not, as an institution, abolished by the advent of the Messiah and the setting up of his kingdom among the Gentile nations.
>
> It furnished then, as now, a standard by which to try existing governments. That it was not intended to induce them to "honor"—and reverence and sustain, the imperial authority of Nero, we have already endeavored to show. They could not so understand it. At first, they might be somewhat surprised— but soon—upon a little reflection, they would see that in these verses the Apostle had really furnished a very clear mirror in which they could see, by contrast, the hideous features of the "beastly" power of Rome.
>
> It presented then, and does now, the specific ends which the godly should seek to attain in their reforming efforts.[8]

The civil government is not different from what we saw in Exodus. There exists an institution possessing the delegated

---

8. James M. Willson, *The Establishment and Limits of Civil Government: An Exposition of Romans 13:1-7* (Powder Springs, GA: American Vision, 2009), 120.

authority of God. It is an institution of representative government with a hierarchy through which to work. The specific
role of the civil government is that of punishing crime with
force up to and including the "use of the sword."

> The magistrate is invested with punitive power. "He beareth
> the sword." This language is partially figurative. The "sword"
> is the emblem of the power of civil government to inflict pains
> and penalties. In this respect, civil authority stands in direct
> and striking contrast to ecclesiastical; for the latter has no oth-
> er power than that which appeals to the understanding, the
> heart and the conscience: it can act by means of admonition,
> reproof, exhortation, and, in the last resort, can place the erro-
> neous and the immoral outside the pale of the visible church.
> Civil authority sustains itself and enforces its enactments by
> penalties of a different sort, when necessary. It uses force, not
> as the only means of securing conformity to its decrees, for
> it also may use admonition and persuasion—but, as the last
> resort, when milder measures fail.[9]

I would only add that the magistrate is directed to use his
sword at the direction of his ruling authority. If he is carrying
out the will of God on earth, then his actions will be governed
by Scripture. If he is carrying out a justice defined by any other
standard than Scripture, then he is knowingly or unknowingly
carrying out the will of another master in opposition to God.

9. Willson, 56.

Matthew 12:30 is instructive at this point: "Whoever is not with me is against me."

STATE SUCCESSION

All people living in community will seek to set up a governing authority that punishes what are perceived to be threats to the livelihood of that community. Satan seeks to set up centralized tyrannies (think Tower of Babel). God seeks to set up decentralized authority. The role of the state is to punish crime according to the character of God as revealed in Scripture. If it misuses this authority, then it is subject to the punishment of the Supreme King.

If it uses it according to the Word of God, then Jesus' rule will be manifested and the community will be blessed. Those living under a pagan state must see themselves like the converted wife discussed above. They should not be content in being subject to godless rule. They should evangelize and teach so that God may regenerate the hearts of many and mounting influence will work its way up through the hierarchy until the officers themselves subject themselves to and begin to reflect the authority of God. If a nation's leaders refuse to represent the one true God, then He will take away their sword.

> Now therefore, O kings, be wise;
> be warned, O rulers of the earth.
> Serve the LORD with fear,
> and rejoice with trembling.
> Kiss the Son,

lest he be angry, and you perish in the way,

for his wrath is quickly kindled.

Blessed are all who take refuge in him. (Ps. 2:10-12)

THE CHURCH

Much like the previous discussions, we need to know where the church begins and how we know it is an institution bound by covenantal oath, representing God's authority and carrying out His rule on earth. Where was the church established in Scripture? What are the bounds of her authority? What are the lawful sanctions it can carry out and how does it continue here on earth and into eternity? Before we get to those questions, we need to clarify something. The focus in this section will be on the earthly institution versus what is sometimes referred to as the invisible church, eschatological church, or elect of God that have their names inscribed in the Lamb's Book of Life.

The reason these two are not the same on earth is obvious. We cannot discern the heart. God tells us that there are those that will fall away and even states in 2 Peter that

> false prophets also arose among the people, just as there will be false teachers among you, who will secretly bring in destructive heresies, even denying the Master who bought them, bringing upon themselves swift destruction. And many will follow their sensuality, and because of them the way of truth will be blasphemed. (2 Peter 2:1-2)

Again in 2 John 2:19 we see "they went out from us, but they were not of us; for if they had been of us, they would have continued with us. But they went out, that it might become plain that they all are not of us." To say that they did not continue with the church because they were godless and unrepentant is not to say that they did not have membership with the people of God at some point in time.

Through our imperfect judgment we are to govern rolls of the church on earth to reflect the perfect judgment of God and His membership roll in heaven. Those who will continue in communion with God into eternity will be those who not only "confess with their mouth," but those who "believe in their heart." God has told us that only He can see the heart. Yet, we are left with what we have. This is the institutional church. Let's look more closely at what exactly we mean by this.

THE CHURCH ESTABLISHED

Those of us who have grown up in the church have often heard the phrase, "The church is not the building, but the people inside the building."[10] Although the phrase is helpful for some clarification, what does it really mean? What defines the people as the church? If we have to have an indicator outside of the heart of man, what is it? Since the answer to these questions and extensive discussion on the church was given in

---

10. God's covenant with His people began before the foundation of the world. His plan and covenant were in place before time began. We see it first manifested in history with Adam and Eve in the garden following the Fall.

chapter 1, I will summarize and then comment a bit more on the jurisdiction and authority of the church.

Creation is fallen and in need of redemption—all of creation. God is not only in the process of redeeming a people to Himself, but of restoring all creation. He does this through individuals and institutions. We see His redemptive and restorative actions carried out through a covenant. The supreme suzerain (conquering king) comes to the enemy people (fallen mankind) and extends a peace treaty or covenant. Those under the covenant are now subjects and servants and are subject to the terms of the covenant.

As described earlier, the terms are outlined in Scripture alone. We see His subjects entering into covenant throughout history—Adam, Noah, Abraham, Jacob, Moses, and David. The same covenant is extended through the church. God extends His hand to the Gentiles in the New Covenant. The church (in the New Covenant), along with all of these mentioned, are manifestations of this one treaty of peace offered by the supreme King, who is Jesus Christ.

As we have seen above, families and even nations can place themselves in covenant with God. There is one covenant with one law (Scripture) and multiple institutions (governments) that have specific jurisdictional authority and unique sanctions as the will of God is worked out on earth "as it is in heaven."

So, when was the "church" covenant established? Although we have to go back to Genesis to see the first picture of the church (as we will discuss later), I will leave it to Douglas Wilson to comment on the early establishment of the church:

Near the beginning of our redemptive history, the Lord God came to Abraham and graciously made an *everlasting* covenant with him (Gen. 17:7, 13). God, who cannot lie or change, sealed this covenant with Abraham in an oath, taken in His own name, so that *believers throughout all history* might have strong consolation (Heb. 6:18). Since there was no one greater to swear by, God swore to this covenant by Himself, because He had determined to show the heirs of promise that this everlasting covenant was indeed *everlasting,* and that His counsel in this matter was *immutable* (Heb. 6:13-14, 17-18). The covenant with Abraham, confirmed to him *in Christ,* was a covenant which by its very nature could not be annulled (Gal. 3:17). We can see how God has fulfilled His promise to Abraham; it is by the blood of this everlasting covenant that we as Christians are saved (Heb. 13:20). The covenant made with Abraham is still in force today; this glorious covenant made with Abraham millennia ago is nothing other than the *new* covenant.[11]

The church of Jesus Christ is built on the apostles and the prophets, with Christ being the chief cornerstone. Peter confessed the name of Christ and was told by Jesus that it was on him or his confession that He would build His church. Later, Peter told the inquiring Jewish people at Pentecost that they must repent and be baptized in the name of Jesus as the Messiah (Acts 2:37–38). We see the building of the church clearly in Acts 2:41 as many place themselves under the New

11. Douglas Wilson, *To a Thousand Generations: Infant Baptism: Covenant Mercy for the People of God* (Moscow, ID: Canon Press, 1996), 115.

Covenant. The church was established and is defined as those placing themselves in covenant with God under the authority of the church.

CHURCH AUTHORITY

The church operates under the authority of Jesus Christ. It is through the church that God's people commune in peace with Him at His table. The first picture of this authority and communion is in the book of Genesis.

> After Abraham's return from the defeat of Chedorlaomer and the kings who were with him, the king of Sodom went out to meet him at the Valley of Shaveh (that is, the King's Valley). And Melchizedek king of Salem brought out bread and wine. (He was Priest of God Most High.) And he blessed him and said, "Blessed be Abram by God Most High, possessor of heaven and earth; and blessed be God Most High, who has delivered your enemies into your hand!" And Abram gave him a tenth of everything. (Gen. 14:17-20)

Jesus' authority comes directly from the Father. In Hebrews we read:

> So also Christ did not exalt himself to be made a high priest, but was appointed by him who said to him, "You are my Son, today I have begotten you"; as he says also in another place, "You are a priest forever, after the order of Melchizedek."

In the days of his flesh, Jesus offered up prayers and supplica-
tions, with loud cries and tears, to him who was able to save
him from death, and he was heard because of his reverence.
Although he was a son, he learned obedience through what
he suffered. And being made perfect, he became the source
of eternal salvation to all who obey him, being designated by
God a high priest after the order of Melchizedek. (Heb. 5:5-10)

The church is subject to the authority of the High Priest,
Jesus Christ. Keep in mind that the quotation above regarding
the establishment of the church with Abraham while you read
the following section from Hebrews.

For this Melchizedek, king of Salem, priest of the Most High
God, met Abraham returning from the slaughter of the kings
and blessed him, and to him Abraham apportioned a tenth
part of everything. He is first, by translation of his name, king
of righteousness, and then he is also king of Salem, that is,
king of peace. He is without father or mother or genealogy,
having neither beginning of days nor end of life, but resem-
bling the Son of God he continues a priest forever.

See how great this man was to whom Abraham the patri-
arch gave a tenth of the spoils! And those descendants of Levi
who receive the priestly office have a commandment in the
law to take tithes from the people, that is, from their brothers,
though these also are descended from Abraham. But this man
who does not have his descent from them received tithes from
Abraham and blessed him who had the promises. It is beyond

dispute that the inferior is blessed by the superior. In the one
case tithes are received by mortal men, but in the other case,
by one of whom it is testified that he lives. One might even
say that Levi himself, who receives tithes, paid tithes through
Abraham, for he was still in the loins of his ancestor when
Melchizedek met him. (Heb. 7:1-10)

Abraham was under the authority of and was blessed by
the priest of the Most High God. The church then and the
church now are both under the eternal covenant (Heb. 13:20)
and acknowledge Jesus' authority, as well as have opportunity
to be blessed by Him (Heb. 7:1, 6) by sitting at His table and
eating bread and drinking wine (Gen. 14:18; Luke 22:19-20).

As we see throughout the New Testament, Jesus delegates
His authority to leaders within the church that govern the
body according to the terms of the covenant (Matt. 16:19).

"If your brother sins against you, go and tell him his fault, between you and him alone. If he listens to you, you have gained
your brother. But if he does not listen, take one or two others
along with you, that every charge may be established by the
evidence of two or three witnesses. If he refuses to listen to
them, tell it to the church. And if he refuses to listen even to
the church, let him be to you as a Gentile and a tax collector.
Truly, I say to you, whatever you bind on earth shall be bound
in heaven, and whatever you loose on earth shall be loosed in
heaven. Again I say to you, if two of you agree on earth about
anything they ask, it will be done for them by my Father in

heaven. For where two or three are gathered in my name, there am I among them." (Matt. 18:15-20)

This passage is the basis of the church's authority on earth. Whereas the family has the rod and the civil ruler has the sword, the church is the only institution that is given the power to curse and remove from the earthly fellowship. This curse and removal from fellowship serve as a warning to the unrepentant, should they not repent, that they are in danger of being forever cut off from God's table in heaven. Paul uses the phrase "delivering over to Satan" (1 Cor. 5:5; 1 Tim. 1:20). This is the final sanction brought against the oath-taker for breaking the terms of his vow to God through the church. Prior to this final sanction there is ongoing reproof through the preaching of God's Word as well as instructions for specific reproof in private and then in public among witnesses. The church exercises Christ's authority against breaking the terms of the covenant.

Confession guards the entrance into the church and baptism is the sign and seal of the covenant and communion at the Lord's table that marks out the boundary line of the church. The church accepts a covenant member on Trinitarian confession and disciplines according to Scripture, which at times calls for the excommunication of the unrepentant. The blessings of those that keep covenant in the church are as numerous as the blessings for obedience in the other two institutions as well as individually in all of life.

CHURCH SUCCESSION

Of all three institutions, the true church is the only one to extend into eternity. Not all members of the visible or historical church on earth will enter into eternity, but only those with true faith called by God who persevere until the end. Revelation 2:7 says, "To the one who conquers I will grant to eat of the tree of life, which is in the paradise of God."

In Revelation 21 we see "the Bride, the wife of the Lamb." Verse 27 says of the New Jerusalem that those who enter it will be "only those who are written in the Lamb's book of life." Until that day, the church on earth is to be governed in such a way that her rolls reflect the roll in heaven. History displays the maturation of God's kingdom. Over time and through the power of the Holy Spirit, men covenantally bound to God exercise better judgment in the affairs of life. Only God executes perfect judgment, but He calls His servants to exercise judgment on earth in His name. The extent of human imperfection in executing justice will reflect itself on the church rolls. This should accent the need for all churchmen to study the Scripture all the more and pray for the help of the Holy Spirit. As we get closer to the consummation of the marriage between Christ and His bride, we will see the church grow in her ability to govern as Christ would. On the final day, He will execute His perfect justice and those in true fellowship with Him will sit down at His table for eternity.

SUMMARY AND CONCLUSION

There has been an epic battle for the hearts of men and the kingdoms of the earth. There are only two sides on which to fight. "You cannot drink the cup of the Lord and the cup of demons; you cannot partake of the table of the Lord and the table of demons" (1 Cor. 10:21). Satan definitively lost the battle at the cross. "He disarmed the rulers and authorities and put them to open shame, by triumphing over them in him" (Col. 2:15). His struggles until the end of time will be in vain. Yet, in history men represent one of the two sides with every thought and action. Men take corporate responsibility and either govern according to the Word of God or according to their fallen nature.

God has ordained a covenant structure in which men are bound to Him judicially and carry out His will in all areas of life. This judicial bond is sealed by an oath. An oath acknowledges His authority and calls down His blessings and curses for either keeping or breaking the terms of the covenant. There is one primary covenant that serves as a peace treaty between God and fallen man. That everlasting covenant has been expressed throughout history ever since God provided a covering for Adam and Eve in the garden following their sin. The covenant was conditional. The death of Jesus Christ as an atoning sacrifice for sin satisfied the terms of the covenant for His people.

This covenant manifests itself on earth through visible institutions. There is in fact one King offering terms of peace with His vassals. There is one peace treaty offered by Jesus through His church. There is one law. There are multiple institutions with separate jurisdictions and unique sanctions to carry out the rule of the supreme ruler who is Jesus sitting at the right hand of the Father.

We have three examples of institutions or governments that can covenant with God and bring about justice according to His law. In Scripture we see the marriage or family covenant, the church covenant, and the civil or state covenant. There is no evidence that these institutions or their ability to place themselves in covenant with God have been done away with.

> And, hence, the Most High has invested all his institutions with some degree of restraining power; and has given them laws by which they are to be guided in the disciplinary or punitive department of their functions. In this sense, parents are "ministers of God," in the training of their children—church officers in the exercise of discipline, and, now, we add, civil rulers in the inflictions of penal law. "Servants of God;" for they act by his authority, and are limited and directed by his supreme and sovereign enactments.[12]

Whereas most would acknowledge that a family and church can be covenanted together under God, some do not so readily think of the state in such terms. This is not to say that the state is neutral in terms of God's rule and that such a realm belongs only to Satan. The state can and should covenantally subject itself to Jesus Christ.

Some might argue that if all three institutions come under the rule of Christ, it creates a recipe for tyranny. To the contrary,

12. Willson, 58.

such a situation limits the tyranny of Satan. We know all too well of the tyranny of the church in history. We also know of the tyranny of the state as well as family dynasties. When fused together in any combination there is opportunity for absolute rule and tyranny by autonomous man, as with the Tower of Babel. This is altogether different from one revealed law governing all three institutions with different jurisdictions and unique powers of rule and sanction that in fact *limit* by design the opportunity for human tyrants to rise and rule contrary to God's law.

The truth is, irrespective of when they think is appropriate in history, all Christians argue for the rule of God at some point in time. They agree with 1 Corinthians 15:25 when it says, "For he must reign until he has put all his enemies under his feet." The answer to when is determined by one's view of the power of the Holy Spirit on earth as well as their understanding of "your [God's] will be done, on earth as it is in heaven."

The remainder of this book will focus on the institution of the church and specifically the sign and seal of the covenant with the church. The church cannot be fully understood without an understanding of a biblical covenant, nor can it be understood outside of the context of all three institutions God has ordained to carry out His justice on earth.

The first two chapters were intended to be a brief overview of these ideas. There are those much more qualified than I am to discuss them further, but they should provide a lens through which we can obtain a better picture of the entrance into the church on earth as well as the accompanying sign of such covenanted membership.

CHAPTER THREE:

COVENANT STRUCTURE AND CHILDREN IN THE OLD TESTAMENT

WE ARE ALMOST TO THE POINT WHERE WE can begin to discuss baptism more specifically. My intention so far has been to provide a context and framework necessary for such a discussion. Without a comprehensive biblical paradigm through which to understand important theological issues, we are in danger of leaning too much on traditions or worse, building good cases on what we might call sandy presuppositions. I am light-years from putting forth a comprehensive paradigm in the first two chapters, but I am hopeful that the reader has a better understanding of the fundamental biblical concept of the covenant.

Without a basic understanding of how the Creator relates to His creation, we cannot even begin a fruitful discussion on the nature of the church and her members. God relates to all of His creation through a personal but legal, rather than a mystical, connection called a covenant. Adam broke the covenant at creation. The wages, or sanction deserved for this sin, is death. Because of the sin of Adam, all men are born in sin. All men are born as enemies of God, rebellious in nature.

God, the sovereign, all-powerful, and just ruler of all creation, comes into history as a conquering King, offering to this rebellious people a peace treaty—a covenant which, if entered into, requires their full allegiance according to its terms. It gives them an opportunity to be reconciled to their Creator. They are to act as vassals carrying out the will of the Great King on earth and act or judge in terms of His law.

One major problem is that, in their rebellious nature, no one is capable of surrendering on their own. As a provision and according to the good pleasure of the King, He provides grace to His people by opening their eyes and giving them the power to submit themselves to Him. In doing so, they confess He is Lord and subject themselves to His rule. Through His power they are able to rule as vassals and help carry out His will on earth as it is done in heaven.

The change of heart wrought by the power of the King is not clearly discernible to other men but is vaguely discernible through outward actions. Put another way, no man knows another man's thoughts and intentions. He can only visibly appraise or judge other men through the way they act in terms of the stipulations of the treaty.

So, inevitably, on earth we have the odd but perhaps common swearing of allegiance to the Great King for reasons other than true devotion. Men in fact can enter into the visible, objective covenant on earth through confession and yet still have a rebellious heart. This heart may reveal itself over time and at the end of time it will be fully revealed. The Great King in His all-knowing nature will finally take all men with a rebellious nature and purge them from His kingdom so that blessings of eternal life and glory can be enjoyed by His faithful subjects. This is the idea of God's covenant in history.

Following the discussion on the idea of a covenant, we looked at how this legal bonding took place in history. God's Word provides us with an understanding of three covenant institutions with three separate and limited jurisdictions. Each can be covenanted to God. Each has a head. Each has a ruling hierarchy. Each is governed under the one revealed law, the Word of God. Each carries out sanctions in their jurisdiction as prescribed by that law. Each institution represents its subjects to God and God to its subjects.

As shown in the first chapter, God's covenant with His people began the day He made provision for a covering for Adam and Eve. In His grace He began a work to redeem a people to Himself. We saw that redemptive covenant take definite shape when God entered into a covenant with Abraham. When God entered into this covenant with Abraham, He accompanied the act with a sign and seal.

Before we discuss at length what is signified and what is sealed, let's for now stress that Abraham was under the terms of a covenant and God placed a mark of ownership upon him. What I will focus on in this chapter is not only what such a mark meant but also the fact that God's marriage and family covenant structure required that it be put on Abraham's household. Within God's intended covenant structure for the family, the father's status as a vassal necessarily gave his children status as subjects as well.

COVENANT STRUCTURE

In the previous chapter, we discussed in depth the family as a covenant institution. It is a corporate body (two or more), legally bound to God. This body has a head who is the husband. The wife was created as a helpmeet, that is, specifically designed to be suitable for him as they exercise dominion in God's name. As such, she is not ethically inferior but is functionally and covenantally submissive in helping the head in his labor of subduing the earth.

Also in the family hierarchy, the children are subjects and are to submit to their parents for the purpose of being raised in the fear and admonition of the Lord. "And these words that I command you today shall be on your heart. You shall teach them diligently to your children, and shall talk of them when you sit in your house, and when you walk by the way, and when you lie down, and when you rise" (Deut. 6:6-7). One day these children will leave and be bound to God within their own families. "Therefore a man shall leave his father and his mother and hold fast to his wife, and they shall become one flesh" (Gen. 2:22–24). And so it goes, family by family reproducing faithful subjects that submit to the will of God the Father.

It is important to remember that though each family is made up of individuals, the family itself is a corporate body bound to God. God related to these families as such. We see this throughout the Old Testament. Following Adam we see God blessing the family of Noah. As the father goes, so goes his household. Noah and his family were saved in the ark. God then made a covenant with him, and it encompassed his off-spring. "Behold, I establish my covenant with you and your offspring after you" (Gen. 9:9).

As we have seen, the same was true with Abraham and his family. God's blessings were distributed to the households of obedient adults. "But the steadfast love of the LORD is from everlasting to everlasting on those who fear him, and his righteousness to children's children, to those who keep his covenant and remember to do his commandments" (Ps. 103:17–18).

God's chastening also was given to families. "You shall not bow down to them or serve them, for I the LORD your God am a jealous God, visiting the iniquity of the fathers on the children to the third and the fourth generation of those who hate me" (Exod. 20:5).

It is obvious how the family functioned as a corporate body. Children in the Old Testament legally belonged to their parents. Intuitively we know that we cannot separate who a child becomes from the identity and practice of their mother and father (assuming, in fact, that they are a household that functions together as a family). Children share the experiences of their parents. Old Testament families lived, worked, and feasted together. If a father denied Jehovah as the one true God, His children would suffer because of the father's decision. Likewise, if a father and mother faithfully followed God, their children would benefit. This did not stop with the children. We also see that in Israel, as soon as servants joined a Hebrew household, they were included covenantally:

> [B]oth he who is born in your house and he who is bought with your money, shall surely be circumcised. So shall my covenant be in your flesh an everlasting covenant. (Gen. 17:13)

> And the LORD said to Moses and Aaron, "This is the statute of the Passover: no foreigner shall eat of it, but every slave that is bought for money may eat of it after you have circumcised him." (Exod. 12:43–44)

The covenant institution of the family was not bound by blood, but by covenant. The household was a covenanted corporate entity that could itself covenant with God. The covenant head with his authority could confess Jehovah as Lord and place himself and his household under the terms of the covenant with God. As goes the head, so goes the household.

OLD TESTAMENT CIRCUMCISION

With this in mind, we should not be surprised that the sign and seal of Abraham's covenant with God was given to his sons. As subjects of their father, they too were bound to Jehovah. This is family solidarity. So what was this circumcision all about?

In Scripture we see that when oaths are taken and covenants are solemnized, they are accompanied by sacrifice, a meal, or some other act of significance which celebrates, signifies, or seals the covenant. Like a conquering king who seals a peace treaty with his signet, God chose circumcision as the sign and seal of His covenant with Abraham. Chapters 12–17 of Genesis detail God's covenant with Abraham. In chapter 17 we first read of the act of circumcision:

> When Abram was ninety-nine years old the LORD appeared to Abram and said to him, "I am God Almighty; walk before me, and be blameless, that I may make my covenant between me and you, and may multiply you greatly." Then Abram fell on his face. And God said to him, "Behold, my covenant is with you, and you shall be the father of a multitude of nations. No longer shall your name be called Abram, but your name shall be Abraham, for I have made you the father of a multitude of nations. I will make you exceedingly fruitful, and I will make you into nations, and kings shall come from you. And I will establish my covenant between me and you and your offspring after you throughout their generations for an everlasting covenant, to be God to you and to your offspring after you. And I will give to you and to your offspring after you the land of your sojournings, all the land of Canaan, for an everlasting possession, and I will be their God."

And God said to Abraham, "As for you, you shall keep my covenant, you and your offspring after you throughout their generations. This is my covenant, which you shall keep, between me and you and your offspring after you: Every male among you shall be circumcised. You shall be circumcised in the flesh of your foreskins, and it shall be a sign of the covenant between me and you. He who is eight days old among you shall be circumcised. Every male throughout your generations, whether born in your house or bought with your money from any foreigner who is not of your offspring, both he who is born in your house and he who is bought with your money, shall surely be circumcised. So shall my covenant be in your flesh an everlasting covenant. Any uncircumcised male who is not circumcised in the flesh of his foreskin shall be cut off from his people; he has broken my covenant." (vv. 1–14)

In this passage we see God's covenant sign applied not only to the head Abraham, but to his whole household. This would be in line with our understanding of God's covenant institution, the family. So what did this covenantal act do for Abraham and his family? What was the purpose? What did it all mean? Why was it so important?

First, circumcision signifies the need for purification of our defiled nature. None of Adam's children are acceptable to God. They are all unclean and defiled. The male genital organ is used to initiate the giving of another life here on earth. God's choice of circumcision drives home that if this organ is unclean, then nothing clean can come from it. There is no natural hope in and for humanity. Left to ourselves we breed defilement and cannot produce anything acceptable to God.

Circumcision is the cutting away of the foreskin of the male genital organ that denotes cleanliness. Jeremiah gives us further insight into this aspect of purification. "Circumcise yourselves to the LORD; remove the foreskin of your hearts, O men of Judah and inhabitants of Jerusalem" (Jer. 4:4). Man is dirty and needs to be cleansed to be acceptable to God.

Understandably then, this covenant sign points to Jesus Christ and His finished work on the cross as the only hope for defiled man. Although those in the Old Testament did not have the benefit of the full revelation of God, we do:

> And you, who were dead in your trespasses and the uncircumcision of your flesh, God made alive together with him, having forgiven us all our trespasses, by canceling the record of debt that stood against us with its legal demands. This he set aside, nailing it to the cross. (Col. 2:13-14)

From here it is important to understand that circumcision did not signify the faith or purified status of the recipient. It signified their need for purification from their defilement and the faith that is imputed by Jesus Christ for the forgiveness of sins. This truth is evident in that many persons were commanded to be circumcised in the Old Testament whom God knew would not be recipients of His grace. Yet God's saving work was as clearly pictured in Ishmael's circumcision as it was in

Abraham's. The picture was the same. Paul picks up this point in Romans 4:

> Is this blessing then only for the circumcised, or also for the uncircumcised? For we say that faith was counted to Abraham as righteousness. How then was it counted to him? Was it before or after he had been circumcised? It was not after, but before he was circumcised. He received the sign of circumcision as a seal of the righteousness that he had by faith while he was still uncircumcised. The purpose was to make him the father of all who believe without being circumcised, so that righteousness would be counted to them as well. (vv. 9-11)

Douglas Wilson's comments on this passage speak clearly:

> It would be hard for Paul to make his point any more clearly. Abraham was declared righteous in the eyes of God *through his faith*. Abraham then received the sign of that righteousness, circumcision. Thus, we see that when Abraham was declared righteous by God, his heart was circumcised. Years later, he was physically circumcised as a sign. Paul says that Abraham received the *sign* of circumcision, which was also a *seal* of the righteousness he had by faith. This was a seal, *not of Abraham's faith*, but of the righteousness which he had *by* faith. Abraham's righteousness was not his own personal faith; his righteousness was Christ, whom he appropriated *by* faith. Thus, *the seal of circumcision was not a seal given as a personal testimony*. The seal was God's seal of the promised

and coming Christ, in whom Abraham believed. The meaning of Abraham's circumcision was not, "Abraham got saved."
Rather, it was, "Salvation will come to the world!" It is true
that Abraham was personally saved, and that he was saved by
faith. But he was saved because he believed in the objective
promise—that is, in the coming Christ.[1]

In addition to purification from defilement through a
coming Savior, circumcision also signifies a boundary between
God's covenant people and the world. Exodus 12:48 states, "If
a stranger shall sojourn with you and would keep the Passover
to the LORD, let all his males be circumcised. Then he may
come near and keep it; he shall be as a native of the land. But
no uncircumcised person shall eat of it."

God's people were marked out from the world through
circumcision and the corporate or covenantal nature of their
households. They were distinguished from those that were not
vassals of God Jehovah. They were holy and set apart. Strangers
could enter the covenant through confession and submission
just as there was the possibility of being cut off from God's
covenant people.

> Thus, in symbolizing the curse on the covenant-breaker, cir-
> cumcision included a reference to the cutting off of one's
> descendants and so of one's name and future place in the
> covenant community. However, insofar as circumcision was a

1. Douglas Wilson, *To a Thousand Generations* (Moscow, ID: Canon Press,
1996), 43.

sign of consecration, it signified that the issue of the circumcised member was consecrated to the Lord of the covenant
and thereby set aside from profane to holy status, that is, to
membership in the covenant institution.[2]

Finally, circumcision signified God's ownership of His people
and their covenantal union and communion with Him.

> And I will establish my covenant between me and you and
> your offspring after you throughout their generations for an
> everlasting covenant, to be God to you and to your offspring
> after you. (Gen. 17:7)

> I will take you to be my people, and I will be your God, and
> you shall know that I am the LORD your God, who has brought
> you out from under the burdens of the Egyptians. (Exod. 6:7)

It is certainly true that God is the God of all men in the sense
that He created them and they are responsible before their
Creator. At the same time, God establishes a special relationship with His people in the New Testament for the purposes
of His glory and carrying out His redemptive plan among all
of His created order. He gives them the benefit of His direct
revelation. He takes them to be His bride and His people are
special to Him. He relates to them differently than the Gentile
world so that He may carry out His redemptive plan in that

2. Meredith G. Kline, *Kingdom Prologue* (South Hamilton, MA: M.G. Kline, 1991), 361.

world. His presence tabernacled among them as a pointer to the coming Holy Spirit. He communed with them at special meals. He was their God, and they were His special people.

One final note about the purpose and meaning of circumcision is the understanding of circumcision's representation of judgment. This is seen in the bloody nature of the rite. There was a penalty to be paid for man's sin. We know from Scripture that the penalty due all of us is death. The death represented in circumcision is the death of the regenerate in Christ Jesus and His death, or the eternal death of the recipient outside of God's saving work. It is a covenantal sign picturing judicial death as the penalty for man's rebellion. By placing themselves (or their households) under the terms of God's peace treaty, they were submitting to Him as King, Lord, and Savior—not only in this life on earth, but also placing themselves at His mercy in death.

> Hence, by circumcision, the sign of the consecratory oath of the Abrahamic Covenant, a man confessed himself to be under the juridical authority of Yahweh and consigned himself to the ordeal of his Lord's judgment for the final verdict on his life. The sign of circumcision thus pointed to the eschatological judicial ordeal with its awful sanctions of eternal weal or woe.[3]

In summary, through circumcision a man and his household were picturing the defilement of fallen man and the coming salvation through Jesus Christ. Through it they were set apart

3. Meredith G. Kline, *By Oath Consigned: A Reinterpretation of the Covenant Signs of Circumcision and Baptism* (Grand Rapids: Eerdmans, 1968), 48.

from the rest of the world for the redemptive purposes of God, and it was a symbol of God's ownership of His people with which He covenantally communed. As His people, they were consigned to Him through this bloody rite, acknowledging the deserved death for their sinful state. In addition, it was a sign of judicial life for those adopted by the second Adam. Circumcision was God's chosen pointer to the work of Jesus Christ on the cross.

COVENANT SIGN AND STRUCTURE

God's sign of circumcision was to be given according to His command. In the Old Testament God chose to work through the covenantal inclusion of children. Not only were the male children to be given the sign, but in receipt of such they were bound to God judicially in the same way as their father. The father spoke or confessed for his whole household. God designed that chosen heads of households (not always the father) were to faithfully represent God to their household. In addition, God designed that the head represents his household to God.

This principle of corporate reality comes from the image of God as we are made in His image. This is the nature of the Trinity. God is distinctly three persons with three different roles. The Trinity involves a functional hierarchy of these persons. Yet, these persons are one God. Whether it be the covenantal nature of the family, the church, or the state as we saw in chapter 2, God chooses to relate to people both individually and in covenant. Evil men in Israel benefited at times of God's blessing. In the same way, there were many like Jeremiah who, although faithful, was taken away to Egypt and died due to God's judgment on His people as a whole. This corporate reality is inescapable in the economy of God.

Children in the Old Testament were treated according to God's covenantal design. Many misconstrue the understanding of God's Old Testament people in that they treat God's covenant with them as a racial or national issue. It was a covenantal issue. God works through family. Sons and daughters are de facto covenant children—a passive or inherent legal bond. Servants or adopted children are not de facto but covenantally united on the basis of an active legal bond. God chose to work through the family—not through bloodlines, but through covenant representation.

Abraham was a man with a family. Because of God's covenant household structure, the sign was given to his sons. He chose a man, Abraham. He chose a nation of people, Israel. Yes, God chose a man and chose the household structure, but the thread that bound the people of God and separated them from the world as a priestly nation was not their blood. To say such a thing would be to say that the thread or unifying agent was genetic. Biological procreation did not determine the boundaries of God's people. God's was a judicial boundary. God used this covenant structure to bring forth in time His promised redeemer, Jesus Christ. Christ's was not a natural bloodline descent but rather a judicial family line carried forward through the redemptive history of His covenant people.

Children in the Old Testament were included in the covenant community through the confession of their head.

Through either having been consigned himself or through his active confession, the head of the family consigned all those legally belonging to him to God. He and his household lived under the terms of the covenant. He also held a responsibility to teach those under his headship how to live in terms of such. He was in fact to produce covenant-keepers over time. Meredith Kline explains it well:

> [T]he parental authority of the confessors of the covenant faith defines the bounds of the covenant community. Those under that parental authority are to be consigned to the congregation. By divine appointment it is the duty of the one who enters God's covenant to exercise his parental authority by bringing those under that authority with himself under the covenantal jurisdiction of the Lord God.[4]

4. Kline, *Kingdom Prologue*, 362.

CHAPTER 4:
COVENANT STRUCTURE AND CHILDREN IN THE NEW TESTAMENT

WITH A BETTER UNDERSTANDING OF GOD'S covenant structure, His three ordained governmental institutions, and His example of how the family and His covenant community interacted in the Old Testament, we can turn our attention to the subject of baptism and the nature of God's covenant people with the coming of Jesus Christ. Since chapter 1 introduced the covenant concept and the two chapters following reviewed it in detail, I will move straight to a discussion of children and covenant structure in the New Testament.

Has there been a change in covenant structure with the coming of Jesus? Is covenant representation still at work? What is baptism? Who are God's New Covenant people and what does this mean? These are the questions I will address in this chapter.

CONTINUITY IN COVENANT STRUCTURE

It is clear from the New Testament that there has not been a significant break with the structure of the family in general. With the coming of Jesus we do not see a change in the functional hierarchy of the family or in the overall task given to the family.

> For man was not made from woman, but woman from man.
> Neither was man created for woman, but woman for man.
> That is why a wife ought to have a symbol of authority on her
> head, because of the angels. Nevertheless, in the Lord woman
> is not independent of man nor man of woman; for as woman
> was made from man, so man is now born of woman. And all
> things are from God. (1 Cor. 11:8–12)

Paul hearkens back to the creation and ensures that we understand that nothing has changed with God's original family structure. It pictures interdependence and synergy in carrying out God's will.

> Wives, submit to your own husbands, as to the Lord. For the
> husband is the head of the wife even as Christ is the head of
> the church, his body, and is himself its Savior. Now as the
> church submits to Christ, so also wives should submit in every-
> thing to their husbands. Husbands, love your wives, as Christ
> loved the church and gave himself up for her, that he might

sanctify her, having cleansed her by the washing of water with the word, so that he might present the church to himself in splendor, without spot or wrinkle or any such thing, that she might be holy and without blemish. In the same way husbands should love their wives as their own bodies. He who loves his wife loves himself. For no one ever hated his own flesh, but nourishes and cherishes it, just as Christ does the church, because we are members of his body. "Therefore a man shall leave his father and mother and hold fast to his wife, and the two shall become one flesh." (Eph. 5:22-31)

Again we see Paul taking us back to Genesis to ensure we understand that the family stands alone as a covenanted body with a purpose. He not only calls out the functional subordination but also provides instruction in regards to how the structure should relate.

Wives, submit to your husbands, as is fitting in the Lord. Husbands, love your wives, and do not be harsh with them. Children, obey your parents in everything, for this pleases the Lord. Fathers, do not provoke your children, lest they become discouraged. Bondservants, obey in everything those who are your earthly masters, not by way of eyeservice, as people-pleasers, but with sincerity of heart, fearing the Lord. Whatever you do, work heartily, as for the Lord and not for men, knowing that from the Lord you will receive the inheritance as your reward. You are serving the Lord Christ. (Col. 3:18-24)

Just as we see in the Old Testament, the family structure is a household structure that extends to and includes both the children and servants functioning as members of the home. Paul also takes the opportunity to make clear who these husbands and masters represent. Any functional subordinate along with their head is serving the Lord Jesus Christ as King over all creation. The head is to represent Jesus to his household and his household to Christ. Every person is responsible individually to God. This personal responsibility is carried out in the place God has put them.

Beyond this, it is all for a purpose, which was clear to Adam and Eve. "And God blessed them. And God said to them, 'Be fruitful and multiply and fill the earth and subdue it, and have dominion over the fish of the sea and over the birds of the heavens and over every living thing that moves on the earth'" (Gen. 1:28). This mandate was issued to Noah and his family as well following the flood. Chapter 6 touches on this concept more completely, but God is, over time, "putting all of his enemies under his feet." However one believes this gets worked out in history, we can all agree that God is ruler over all creation and intends for this to be the program throughout eternity. In the New Testament we see Jesus coming and under His authority commanding a global program of extending His rule. We call this the Great Commission:

> And Jesus came and said to them, "All authority in heaven and on earth has been given to me. Go therefore and make disciples of all nations, baptizing them in the name of the Father

and of the Son and of the Holy Spirit, teaching them to observe all that I have commanded you. And behold, I am with you always, to the end of the age." (Matt. 28:18–20)

Bringing the world into covenant with God through evangelism and teaching obedience to His commands can be nothing other than establishing His rule on earth. Subduing the earth to the authority of Christ is consistent with the original mandate given to Adam and Eve. How are they to carry out this mandate? Since the family has not changed with the coming of Christ, God's intent is to work within the structure of the family. Beyond just the family, Jesus as head is to work through His covenant institutions of family, church, and state to carry out His will in history, leading up to the end of time and the consummation of marriage with His covenant bride, the Church. We saw from chapter 2 that Christ's Church is the only institution that survives into eternity. So, how does the family structure interact with the New Covenant people on earth?

CONTINUITY IN COVENANT INTERACTION
In the Old Testament we have seen that "as goes the head, so goes the household." We also see above that the overall structure of the family has not changed with the coming of Christ. Is there a reason why a child or servant in the Old Testament household could be consigned to the Old Covenant people through the covenant head, but this consignment could not be possible in respect to God's New Covenant people, the church?

We take this continuity for granted in respect to the civil realm. Our children are born to us as citizens of the nation in which we hold our citizenship from birth. They are not excluded in a neutral or non-citizen status until they are old enough to take an oath themselves. They are included on the basis of legal headship. This surely takes on different forms in different cultures, but with remnants of our Christian legal structure we see God's family solidarity still at work.

The book of Hebrews provides some insight into this idea of covenantal consignment through the head. The New Testament author upholds a covenantal argument from the Old Testament, displaying structural continuity:

> See how great this man was to whom Abraham the patriarch gave a tenth of the spoils! And those descendants of Levi who receive the priestly office have a commandment in the law to take tithes from the people, that is, from their brothers, though these also are descended from Abraham. But this man who does not have his descent from them received tithes from Abraham and blessed him who had the promises. It is beyond dispute that the inferior is blessed by the superior. In the one case tithes are received by mortal men, but in the other case, by one of whom it is testified that he lives. One might even say that Levi himself, who receives tithes, paid tithes through Abraham, for he was still in the loins of his ancestor when Melchizedek met him. (Heb. 7:4–10)

Although the greater context of this argument is Jesus Christ and His priesthood over the New Covenant, I want the reader to notice the line of thought in this passage. Melchizedek was bringing the sons of Abraham under his ecclesiastical authority. Abraham was subordinate to Melchizedek. The sons of Levi were subordinate to Abraham. So, the sons of Levi were necessarily subordinate to the order of Melchizedek. The New Testament author is making a covenantal argument from the Old Testament. He wants to demonstrate that the Levitical priesthood is inferior or subordinate to the Melchizedekian priesthood. He does this by tracing the subordination through Abraham. The sons of Levi were consigned to Melchizedek by virtue of their status as heirs.

That our children should be consigned initially to the authority under which the head places himself is made even more clear by the discussions of suzerain-vassal treaties in the first part of this book. The suzerain was a conquering king and his vassals represented his authority in their subordinate kingdoms. Meredith Kline puts it well:

> The suzerain-vassal covenants were authority structures which brought outlying spheres of authority under the sanctioned control of an imperial power.... It is clear then, that these ancient treaties, on the form of which the redemptive covenants were patterned, were engagements not merely between individuals but between broader authority structures. In particular,

the servant king who was bound by the treaty was bound not alone but together with his subjects and his descendants.[1]

There is no reason to believe that this incorporation of covenantal spheres has ceased with the coming of Jesus Christ. He alone is the imperial power who subjects vassals to Himself. These vassals take oaths for themselves and their subjects. It is not only counterintuitive, but seemingly unbiblical to assert a different structure or operation. Before we look into why some might assert differently, let's look at some biblical examples of these covenanting spheres.

When God addressed His covenant people at Sinai through Moses, He addressed the covenanted people as a whole. As the representative elders came before Moses, God instructed the people in the Lord, from babies to grandfathers:

> So Moses came and called the elders of the people and set before them all these words that the LORD had commanded him. All the people answered together and said, "All that the LORD has spoken we will do." And Moses reported the words of the people to the LORD. And the LORD said to Moses, "Behold, I am coming to you in a thick cloud, that the people may hear when I speak with you, and may also believe you forever." (Exod. 19:7–9)

Following this, the Lord spoke through Moses: "And God spoke all these words, saying...." He was addressing the whole

---

1. Meredith G. Kline, *By Oath Consigned: A Reinterpretation of the Covenant Signs of Circumcision and Baptism* (Grand Rapids: Eerdmans, 1972), 84, 86.

people of God. How do we know this included the children? "Honor your father and your mother, that your days may be long in the land that the LORD your God is giving you" (Exod. 20:12). There is perfect continuity between this and Paul's covenant instruction to the church in Ephesus:

> Children, obey your parents in the Lord, for this is right. "Honor your father and mother" (this is the first commandment with a promise), "that it may go well with you and that you may live long in the land." (Eph. 6:1–3)

Paul addresses the church as Moses did the covenant people at Sinai. He spoke to the children as members of the covenant community. He spoke to them in a status different from that of a stranger in the land. They were not strangers in the land. They were bound to God in covenant by virtue of the covenant bond between their head and God Jehovah. We turn again to Kline:

> Another significant fact is that Paul instructed the children of various congregations to obey their parents in the Lord, and in support of his charge cited the pertinent stipulation of the Sinaitic Covenant together with its accompanying covenantal sanction (Eph. 6:1-3, Col. 3:20, cf. Exod. 20:12). Clear confirmation is also found in Paul's directive to covenant parents to bring their children under the nurturing and admonishing authority of the Lord (Eph. 6:4). In this exhortation the apostle takes for granted that it is the very authority of Christ as

covenant Lord that reaches and claims children through the authority of their parents.[2]

Children of confessors are addressed as members of God's covenant people in the New Testament. Rev. M. F. Sadler provides more insight into this in his book, *The Second Adam and the New Birth*. Although I do not subscribe to every position outlined by Sadler, he is helpful with the topic at hand. When speaking of Paul he states the following:

> Now he sends a message to all the children of the Ephesian Christians. "Children, obey your parents in the Lord: for this is right." If the children of the Ephesian Christians had not all been baptized, or if some of them at their Baptism had not really been grafted into the body of Christ's Church, the Apostle must have first laid down how they were to be brought *into* Christ before he could say a word to them about their duties *in* Christ. But he does no such thing. He says not one word about any of these children having to seek an interest in Christ. He says not one word about the necessity laid upon children of being grafted into Christ at some future time, when their faith might be more matured. He takes it for granted that they were growing up in the Church as members of Christ and that the same motives to holiness and goodness which were applicable to the older members of Christ's body were applicable to them in their degree.[3]

2. Kline, *By Oath Consigned*, 94.
3. M. F. Sadler, *The Second Adam and the New Birth: Or, The Doctrine of Baptism as Contained in Holy Scripture* (Monroe, LA: Athanasius Press, 2004), 101.

So why might this idea be so difficult to digest in our present cultural context? Certainly a more complete answer to this question would be extensive and beyond the scope of this present work, but a few brief thoughts may be helpful at this point. Bryan Holstrom, in his book, *Infant Baptism and the Silence of the New Testament*, speaks from a very practical perspective to this question. He speaks to American evangelicalism, which was formed out of the first and second Great Awakenings along with the missionary efforts in carrying the gospel to the western frontier lands. He states,

> The "rugged individualism" of the American frontier tended to shun all expressions of religious authority, whether of the human or written variety. This meant that received traditions were looked on with suspicion (or even contempt), and the private and personal interpretation of the Scriptures was exalted as superior to reliance on the collective wisdom of those who had come before.[4]

He goes on to say,

> As the revivalist emphasis upon conscious conversion only after undergoing an intense emotional struggle was exalted as the normative Christian experience, uncertainty as to the status of children in the covenant became common, which eventually led to a laxity in administering the sacrament to the chil-

4. Bryan D. Holstrom, *Infant Baptism and the Silence of the New Testament* (Greenville, SC: Ambassador International, 2008), 140.

dren of believers.... The new movement was anti-intellectual, anti-clerical, and doggedly individualistic.[5]

Is it any wonder that these ideas of family solidarity and covenant structural continuity are foreign to us? We cannot separate ourselves from the cultural and evangelical context of recent history. We must forever check our current context with the instruction of Scripture so that we may further shape history according to God's will and for His glory. Going back to Scripture for one more illustration of covenanting authority spheres, we must turn to 1 Corinthians 7:12-16:

> To the rest I say (I, not the Lord) that if any brother has a wife who is an unbeliever, and she consents to live with him, he should not divorce her. If any woman has a husband who is an unbeliever, and he consents to live with her, she should not divorce him. For the unbelieving husband is made holy because of his wife, and the unbelieving wife is made holy because of her husband. Otherwise your children would be unclean, but as it is, they are holy. But if the unbelieving partner separates, let it be so. In such cases the brother or sister is not enslaved. God has called you to peace. For how do you know, wife, whether you will save your husband? Or how do you know, husband, whether you will save your wife?

In this passage, Paul is addressing marriage and providing instruction to believers married to unbelievers to remain with

5. Holstrom, *Infant Baptism and the Silence of the New Testament*, 141.

their unbelieving spouse if that spouse is willing to stay in the marriage. Although the New Testament provides grounds for divorce, or "covenantal death," a mere unbelieving spouse is not one of them. Paul then makes a clear statement. He says the unbeliever's status is determined by the commitment of the believing spouse. Whether it be the husband or wife, the marriage is consecrated to God because of the believing spouse. God has covenantally set apart the unbelieving spouse. Paul then mentions the children almost as a passing thought. He makes it clear that the children too are holy or set apart. Their status is one of being bound to God and set apart (the meaning of holy) covenantally. Their status as a believer or unbeliever is not the focus of the passage.

> [T]here does not seem to be any way to construe the holiness ascribed to them other than as a holiness of status.... In what, then, does the holiness of the children's status consist? In accordance with the biblical concept of holiness it will have to involve some sort of dedicatory separation unto the name of God, a consecration to his service and glory. Clearly it is not the holy consecration of subjective spiritual condition.[6]

6. Kline, *By Oath Consigned*, 91-92. Some may notice that this seems to leave room in the church for professing unbelievers. If the children are "set apart" under the sphere of authority of the believing spouse, then so is the spouse as a professing adult. Paul K. Jewett, in *Infant Baptism and the Covenant of Grace* (in my opinion the best work to date on credo-baptism of the ones I have read), tries to solve the issue by saying the believing spouse keeps the unbelieving spouse free from being "contaminated with the taint of illegitimacy" ([Grand Rapids: William B. Eerdmans, 1978], 133-135). Does this mean that all marriages between unbelievers are illegitimate? Clearly marriage has no certain meaning

So we see clearly here that there is complete continuity between the Old and New Testaments regarding covenant structure as well as the interaction between the family structure and
God's New Covenant people. God's people are in covenant
with Him. When one professes Christ, he is bound to Him
along with those within His covenant authority. The sign associated with this covenant bond is baptism. What we find is
that an understanding of baptism follows directly from our
understanding of circumcision discussed in the last chapter.

---

outside of Christ, but such covenant unions are still recognized and function in
society. The issue with this is that it brings a whole new concept into Scripture.
The text clearly says "sanctified" or "made holy." Jewett on page 133 brings in
this notion of being free from defilement. What defilement? What defines or
characterizes defilement, biblically speaking?

Ray Sutton points us to scriptural warrant for understanding the status of
the unbelieving spouse as holy but yet not clean: "The problem concerns the
use of the same word to refer to two different types of sanctification. And, the
problem is further complicated by the fact that the sanctification of the child
makes him clean, whereas no reference is made to the effects of the sanctification of the adult."

"I believe the stranger in the land concept resolves these problems. The
stranger in the land was someone who was generally set apart (sanctified) because he lived in Israel under the law of God and the Sabbath system of festivals.
He did not actually convert to Judaism. Biblical religion is not coercive. It allows
for unbelief in national and social contexts. A man did not have to believe. He
only had to be willing to abide by the law of God in a general, outward sense.

"This general kind of sanctification is carried over to the New Testament.
Paul says to Timothy, 'For everything created by God is good, and nothing is to
be rejected, if it is received with gratitude' (1 Tim. 4:4-5). Like the Old Testament, the application of the Bible has a general sanctifying effect on anything.

"It is in this sense that the unbeliever, married to a believer, is sanctified,
yet not clean. He lives in the sphere of faith. He is the stranger in the home of
the believer." Ray Sutton, "Household Baptisms," Covenant Renewal 2, no. 8
(August 1988): 4: https://bit.ly/1cdIQTS.

NEW TESTAMENT BAPTISM

Baptism is a sign and seal that follows the meaning and purpose of circumcision. The term "sign" is used here just as one might expect. A sign signifies, pictures, or represents a reality. A seal is a legal bond that authenticates the legal relationship. Baptism is, just as circumcision was, a sign and seal of God's covenant.

First, baptism signifies the need for purification of our defiled nature. We are all more than tainted in our flesh. Because of our relationship to the first Adam we come into the world defiled: "And you, who were dead in your trespasses and the uncircumcision of your flesh..." (Col. 2:13). Ananias instructs Paul in the book of Acts to "Rise and be baptized and wash away your sins, calling on his name" (Acts 22:16).

Baptism is a cleansing ritual. It reminds us that we are not clean and represents the need for a washing or purification from such a state. This is an important distinction and one discussed in the previous chapter. Baptism points to the cleansing work of the Holy Spirit. It does not spiritually cleanse the recipient. Rather, it represents that Jesus Christ cleanses the hearts of believers. When a man is baptized this does not declare that "this man was saved," but that "Jesus saves."[7]

Next, baptism declares a setting apart or consecration of the recipient. Baptism signifies a boundary between God's covenant people and the world. Matthew 28 makes it clear that the baptized are set apart with a purpose. Paul takes us

---

7. Of course, if applied in an orthodox Trinitarian church, the recipient is surely saved at that time in terms of being declared as set apart as a covenanted member of God's people on earth.

back to Genesis when he proclaims our consecrated identity: "For as many of you as were baptized into Christ have put on Christ. There is neither Jew nor Greek, there is neither slave nor free, there is no male and female, for you are all one in Christ Jesus. And if you are Christ's, then you are Abraham's offspring, heirs according to promise" (Gal. 3:27–29). It is clear in Romans 6 that our called-out status will be evident in how we walk in life: "We were buried therefore with him by baptism into death, in order that, just as Christ was raised from the dead by the glory of the Father, we too might walk in newness of life" (v. 4).

Scripture refers to Christ's church as saints. They are holy and set apart on the basis of their covenantal relation to God. We have distorted this over time and now use the word "saint" as implying someone with an inner devotion or one who is pure or deeply spiritual from the inside. In doing so we have suffered in our understanding of Scripture and hence our understanding of baptism.

> In no one place is [saint] used to distinguish Christians of very deep holiness and spirituality from those who have not attained to such a measure of conformity to God's will. In only a small number of texts does it imply internal purity and spirituality, and in these places it has reference not to the present character of Christians, but to that which those will be found to possess at Christ's second coming who have continued in that service of Christ to which at Baptism they were solemnly separated and set apart.... In every other place

it is applied to the whole body of baptized Christians in a city
or district and is the continuation of that mode of address
which we find adopted by the Prophets when they called all
Israel a "holy nation"—a people, that is, dedicated to God,
and separated from all other people to serve Him.[8]

In addition to signifying purification and a delineating boundary from the world, Baptism like circumcision also signifies
our union and communion with Christ and His ownership of
us. Matthew 28:19 tells us "Go therefore and make disciples
of all nations, baptizing them in the name of the Father and
of the Son and of the Holy Spirit." We are baptized into the
name of the Trinity. We are clothed with Christ (Gal. 3:27).
This is not a mystical union as we have discussed. It is formal
placement under the stipulations of the New Covenant.[9]

Being placed under the terms of the covenant, we are in
union with Christ. It is a blessed union. It is personal. We relate directly and intimately in covenant with our Creator and
His people. We are members of the church. The picture of this
covenantal union is initiated in baptism and carried forward
in church worship and the Lord's Supper. This union is one in
which we are owned by God. We are slaves to Christ. We are
His people and He is our God.

---

8. *The Second Adam, and the New Birth*, 87, italics in original omitted.

9. Unless I am unclear on his use of certain terms, this is where I take issue
with Sadler's work. He fundamentally sees the sacramental union with Christ
as mystical. He says as much throughout his book, but it is emphasized on pages
220-221. Although full of life, I believe the union is confessional or legal.

A final note about the meaning of baptism would also follow from the last chapter and our discussion about circumcision. Whereas baptism signifies our need for purification, our separation from the world, and our union with the body of Christ, it also pictures the judgment of covenant-breakers. We see this picture in multiple places in the New Testament. It is certainly seen initially in the baptisms of John the Baptist. I will let Kline summarize:

> John the Baptist was sent as a messenger of the Old Covenant to its final generation. His concern was not to prepare the world at large for the coming of Christ but to summon Israel unto the Lord to whom they had sworn allegiance at Sinai, ere his wrath broke upon them and the Mosaic kingdom was terminated in the flames of messianic judgment. The demand which John brought to Israel was focused in this call to baptism. This baptism was not an ordinance to be observed by Israel in their generations but a special sign for that terminal generation epitomizing the particular crisis in covenant history represented by the mission of John as messenger of the Lord's ultimatum.[10]

During John's ministry, his teaching and baptizing, Jesus authorized His disciples in the administration of this baptism described above. An extended quote from Kline is helpful in understanding the significance of picturing judgment in baptism.

10. Kline, *By Oath Consigned*, 61.

He describes further John's mission as a witness and the transition from Old Covenant to New Covenant significance:

> When Jesus began his public ministry, God's lawsuit with Israel was in the ultimatum stage. At this point, the judicial function of Jesus coincided with that of John. Jesus' witness had the effect of confirming John's witness of final warning to Israel... And since the meaning of the baptismal rite administered by these messengers of the covenant derived from the official nature of their mission, the import of Jesus' baptism, though separately conducted, would also be essentially the same as John's. Thus, as a sign of the covenant lawsuit against Israel, the baptismal rite of Jesus was, like John's, a symbol of the imminent judgment ordeal of the people of the Old Covenant. This interpretation of Jesus' early baptizing in terms of the concurrent ultimatum mission of John is strikingly confirmed by the evident cessation of that baptism once John was imprisoned....
>
> When that ultimatum was emphatically rejected, a new phase in the administration of the covenant was entered, Jesus' ministry of baptism ceasing along with the Johannine message of ultimatum which it had sealed.
>
> The difference between the earlier and the later baptisms authorized by Jesus was the difference between two quite distinct periods in the history of the covenant. The later baptism was of course ordained as a sign of the New Covenant; it was not part of the old lawsuit against Israel.

Nevertheless, this new water baptism, appearing so soon after the other and still within the personal ministry of Jesus, would hardly bear a meaning altogether different from the earlier one. There would be a pronounced continuity between Christian baptism and the earlier, Johannine baptism.... It would continue to be a sign of consecration to the Lord of the covenant and, more particularly, a symbolic passage through the judicial ordeal, in which those under the rule of the covenant receive a definitive verdict for eternal glory or for perpetual desolation.[11]

This "symbolic passage through the judicial ordeal" is described clearly by Peter:

[B]ecause they formerly did not obey, when God's patience waited in the days of Noah, while the ark was being prepared, in which a few, that is, eight persons, were brought safely through water. Baptism, which corresponds to this, now saves you, not as a removal of dirt from the body but as an appeal to God for a good conscience, through the resurrection of Jesus Christ. (1 Pet. 3:20–21)

Believers, like Noah, are saved through the waters of judgment. The outward act of cleansing the body does not save, but the inward reality of regeneration through the Holy Spirit does save and this is what the baptism pictures. Nonetheless, it also is a picture of judgment for nonbelievers. The waters

---

11. Kline, *By Oath Consigned*, 63-65.

that saved Noah drowned the rest of creation that would not heed the warning.

The same salvation and judgment through water is pictured elsewhere in the New Testament:

> For I do not want you to be unaware, brothers, that our fathers were all under the cloud, and all passed through the sea, and all were baptized into Moses in the cloud and in the sea, and all ate the same spiritual food, and all drank the same spiritual drink. For they drank from the spiritual Rock that followed them, and the Rock was Christ. (1 Cor. 10:1-4)

It is evident that the water is the instrument of both deliverance and judgment. Paul uses the word "baptism" to describe the event, even though the Israelites were not touched by the water. The water here is clearly not washing God's people. Even so, Paul still uses the term "baptism" to describe their identification with Moses, just as we are now baptized into Christ and are identified with Him in our Christian baptism. For whatever this passage is communicating it is at least another picture of waters of judgment.

It would be good at this time to make a few comments on an essay by Duane Garrett where he sets about to refute Kline's understanding of Christian baptism, and most notably as it has to do with this idea of judgment. Although the essay deserves a more comprehensive response, a few things of note might be observed. Garret states:

The purpose of a water ordeal is to determine guilt or innocence. Neither John's baptism nor any subsequent Christian baptism has this purpose, nor does any biblical text suggest any such thing. People come to be baptized because they know that they are guilty, not to determine guilt or innocence.... Although no one doubts that John's ministry primarily involved warning people of a judgment to come, this does not mean that baptism is an ordeal or a self-imprecatory vow.... In baptism, one acknowledges guilt and the need for forgiveness (that is, one repents).[12]

Garrett presumes what needs proving. The contention of this work is that baptism is not defined as he states it, but rather those that are baptized confess and are put under the stipulations of the covenant. Certainly repentance is wrapped up in this confession. For those that cannot confess, they are consigned to the terms of the covenant by way of their covenant head. This is biblical covenant theology. As to the ordeal itself, let us have Kline speak for himself:

That Peter conceived of Christian baptism as a sign of judicial ordeal is indicated by his likening it to the archetypal water ordeal, the Noachic deluge (1 Pet. 3:20-22). In this passage, ἀντίτυπον (vs. 21) is best taken with βάπτισμα, in which case Christian baptism is directly designated as the antitype of the

12. Duane A. Garrett, "Meredith Kline on Suzerainty, Circumcision, and Baptism," in *Believer's Baptism: Sign of the New Covenant in Christ*, ed. Thomas R. Schreiner and Shawn Wright (Nashville, TN: B&H Academic, 2006), 273-274.

ordeal waters of the deluge, or the passage through those waters. But even if ἀντίτυπον were connected with ὑμᾶς so that
the church would be called the antitype of the Noachic family,
the total comparison drawn by Peter would still involve an interpretation of the baptismal waters in terms of the significance
of the deluge ordeal...the most natural assumption is certainly
that Peter was led to bring the deluge and the rite of baptism
together because of the common element of the waters.[13]

We see here that Kline is emphasizing both the significance of
the deluge ordeal and the common element of the waters of
baptism and of the flood. I do not take him to mean that the
"ordeal meant to determine guilt or innocence"[14] but that the
waters of baptism represent cleansing and salvation or judgment based on the heart of the individual. God tests the heart,
the waters of baptism do not. They merely represent such.

Hebrews 11:7 is further evidence of this representative
saving/judgment aspect of baptism when the writer states, "By
faith Noah, being warned by God concerning events as yet unseen, in reverent fear constructed an ark for the saving of his
household. By this he condemned the world and became an
heir of the righteousness that comes by faith."

God saved Noah through Noah's faith. "Saving" waters of
baptism represent the reward for such faith. Destruction is also
represented through the water—destruction being the sanction
for not abiding by the stipulations of the covenant. This is all

---

13. Kline, *By Oath Consigned*, 65.
14. Garrett, "Meredith Kline on Suzerainty, Circumcision, and Baptism," 274.

very different from the waters of baptism actually functioning mystically as "a test meant to see whether a person is guilty of a charge or not."[15] As evidenced above, I do not understand this to be Kline's position.

The connection between baptism and judgment, or the sanction of death, should not be foreign to us in the New Testament.

> In him also you were circumcised with a circumcision made without hands, by putting off the body of the flesh, by the circumcision of Christ, having been buried with him in baptism, in which you were also raised with him through faith in the powerful working of God, who raised him from the dead. And you, who were dead in your trespasses and the uncircumcision of your flesh, God made alive together with him, having forgiven us all our trespasses.... (Col. 2:11-13)

This circumcision of Christ refers to His death. This death is referred to as a baptism. When a person is baptized it pictures a union with Christ in His death and resurrection to life everlasting. At the very same time it represents the judgment of those not found to be faithful covenant-keepers. The picture is more like that of the deluge during the time of Noah or the drowning of the Egyptian army behind God's people who were in union with Moses.

If baptism represented cleansing only then, it would not be so closely associated with the death of Christ. His death was the punishment for our sin. The waters must necessarily

15. Garrett, "Meredith Kline on Suzerainty, Circumcision, and Baptism," 275.

represent both negative and positive sanctions. Ray Sutton says it well when he states,

> We have already seen in the Great Commission Covenant that baptism is the new sanction. It represents the work of the Holy Spirit. Jesus says, "John baptized with water but you shall be baptized with the Spirit" (Acts 1:5). Paul says, "He saves us, not on the basis of deeds which we have done in righteousness, but according to His mercy, by the washing of regeneration and renewing by the Holy Spirit" (Titus 3:5). We should keep in mind the principle of the Trinity as we read such a passage. The "water" itself does not regenerate, but signifies the incorporation of the believer under the terms of the covenant. It seals the believer covenantally to the Holy Spirit. Baptism warns the baptized: break the terms of the covenant by renouncing Christ, and you will perish by the terms of the covenant. Because baptism is a sanction, there are dual sanctions: blessing and cursing. Baptism seals to Christ, and is in this sense automatic, but it does not automatically create salvation.[16]

In summary, baptism pictures cleansing, consecration, union with Christ, and judgment. This follows closely with circumcision as seen in the previous chapter. When an individual is baptized he or she takes on a sign picturing the cleansing work of the Holy Spirit. It also signifies that they are separate or living holy in this world. They now are counted among those who have a tangible union with the body of Christ on earth.

16. Ray Sutton, *That You May Prosper*, 300-301, italics in original omitted.

As such, they are expected to persevere in their faith and show themselves faithful to the terms of the covenant under which they have placed themselves or to which they have been consigned. If their heart is truly cleansed then they will certainly remain faithful. If they have not undergone a transforming work of the Holy Spirit then they are covenant-breakers and will one day experience the judgment of death, just like the people of Noah's day or the Egyptians who would not submit to the Lord Jehovah.

Does this not mean that the church is comprised of both regenerate and unregenerate people? The answer is, of course that is what it means. That said, if only God knows the heart, then that is necessarily true no matter what someone believes about baptism and the nature of church membership. All churches with a membership roll have a roll with a "mixed membership." This was true of Israel and this is true of the church today. "Covenant member" does not equal "the elect."[17] Stephen Wellum takes issue with this view when he says,

> That is why in a Baptist view of the church, what is unique about the nature of the new covenant community is that it comprises a regenerate, believing people, not a mixed people like Israel of old. Therefore, Baptists only view as true members of the new covenant community those who have actually entered into union with Christ by repentance and faith and as such are

17. Understanding this, we must also understand that we are unable to discern the mysteries of God. We must operate in terms of an objective covenant and treat the members as elect until given reason to think otherwise within the bounds of biblical judicial process.

partakers of all the benefits and blessings of the new covenant age. Furthermore, for Baptists, it is for this reason that baptism, which is the covenant sign of the new covenant church, is reserved for those who have entered into these glorious realities by the sovereign work of God's grace in their lives.[18]

But how can baptism be reserved for "those who have entered into these glorious realities by the sovereign work of God's grace in their lives" if God is the only one who knows this? We have their confession and the way they live their lives as evidence, but we do not have the knowledge of their regenerate status before God. Therefore we baptize on the basis of this confession. By doing this we still have no knowledge of their regenerate status and so we have a membership that we know is "mixed." What Wellum puts forth is impossible to attain in a visible, historical institution. Here it's stated even more clearly: "Because the church, by its very nature, is a regenerate community, the covenant sign of baptism must only be applied to those who have come to faith in Christ."[19] Or, "Scripture teaches that we should only baptize those who are Christ's covenant children—those who are actually in the covenant by God's grace through regeneration and saving faith."[20] If this is what Scripture teaches, it would not be possible to carry out.

Again Wellum says, "But now, in Christ, under his mediation, the relationship between Christ and his seed is no longer

---

18. Stephen J. Wellum, "Baptism and the Relationship Between the Covenants," in *Believer's Baptism: Sign of the New Covenant in Christ*, 113.

19. Wellum, 138.

20. Wellum, 136.

physical but *spiritual*, which entails that the covenant sign must only be applied to those who in fact are the *spiritual* seed of Abraham."[21] The spiritual seed of Abraham are true Israel. They are the elect of God. To say that baptism must only be applied to these is to put credo-baptists (believer's baptism) and paedo-baptists (baptism of infants) in the same position of consistent disobedience. This "must" is not possible on earth in time and space. In a very Gnostic, spiritual sense perhaps it would be possible, but we live in history with an institution requiring earthly covenantal boundaries.

Later in his essay, Wellum drives his position home by stating, "[T]he NT views the church as a *heavenly* (i.e., tied to the 'age to come' and the new creation, not 'in Adam' but 'in Christ') and *spiritual* community (i.e., born of and empowered by the Spirit in faith union with Christ), living her life out now while she awaits the consummation, literally 'the outcropping of the heavenly assembly gathered in the Jerusalem that is above.'"[22] This is all fine, but we live on earth in this age where the boundaries of the church institution are defined by Scripture in a way so as to be visible and tangible. It can be objectively marked out in history.

A common refrain at this point in the argument takes the form of an admission that it is impossible to ensure that only the elect are baptized into an institutional church. In a footnote discussion on the nature of the New Covenant, Wellum says, "Trying to discern true saving faith is merely a human

21. Wellum, 136-137.
22. Wellum, 148-149.

epistemological problem, and we do our best to discern whether one's profession of faith is genuine. But this is a far cry from baptizing where there is no faith."[23]

The discernment mentioned is a problem to the point of being impossible. As to "a far cry from baptizing where there is no faith," I disagree wholeheartedly. This is what we are talking about. Credo-baptists and paedo-baptists alike do in fact end up baptizing where there is not faith. *We have the presence of a confession but the faith must be demonstrated over time.*

The line of thinking in the argument then proceeds to call into question the status of the apostate who once confessed Christ but who came to the point of apostasy. 1 John 2:19 is cited as evidence that there were those that "went out from us" but "were not of us." It is argued that these apostates were somehow among the church but they were never really members of the church or under the terms of the covenant.

Where it may be true that they were never regenerate, someone who confesses and places themselves in covenant is most assuredly a member of something. If this is not the church, then what is it? What are we to call an earthly gathering of professors? Again, is a church only heavenly and invisible? If so, then what is the visible institution? If it is a church, then what defines its boundaries?

The argument that all true apostates were never part of the elect goes without saying. To claim that they were never legally bound to a covenant institution referred to as a church would not make sense. If they were legally bound to an earthly

23. Wellum, 153.

institution called the church then the covenant people on earth are in fact a "mixed" community. More will be covered in the next chapter, but this community, although being comprised of regenerate and unregenerate people, is still a called-out covenant institution. Baptism is the sign of entering into this legal bond. It is nothing less than an incorporation into the church in history.

> Now if the covenant is first and last a declaration of God's Lordship, then the baptismal sign of entrance into it will before all other things be a sign of coming under the jurisdiction of the covenant and particularly under the covenantal dominion of the Lord. Christian baptism is thus the New Covenant sign of consecration or discipleship.[24]

BIBLICAL CHURCH DISCIPLINE AS A NECESSITY

The following is a brief discussion on what I believe to be a cornerstone in this concept of membership in the covenant community called the church. This is not to be confused with the regenerate community of the elect which is indiscernible to us this side of heaven. I will return to a comment from the above section referencing the membership of the church. "We have their confession and the way they live their lives as evidence, but we do not have the knowledge of their regenerate status before God. Therefore we baptize on the basis of this confession." This is incomplete. What needs to be added is

---

24. Kline, *By Oath Consigned*, 79.

that they retain their membership through a life that reflects their confession.

The question of qualification for being incorporated into or retaining membership in the church is most commonly dealt with through two categories of response. One might be labeled rational standards and the other experiential standards.[25] Rational standards for church membership would be based on some measure of intellectual ascent. In some church circles, for younger candidates this ties directly into the notion of an age of accountability. It is thought, if they are smart enough to understand, then they are liable for their sin. Many a Reformed Baptist who may not buy into this from the standpoint of salvation will travel down this road in regards to church membership. From a rational or intellectual standpoint they require the passing of a test of some sort. For children this may take the form of quizzing on doctrinal questions or requiring the memorization of some body of knowledge. For the adult it would take a similar form. This is a rational test. The resulting question is what questions make for a sufficient quiz? How much knowledge is enough to qualify someone for baptism and church membership? In this category faith is intellectual.

The category of experiential standards for baptism and church membership center around testimonies of experience. One capable of articulating a suitable conversion experience can qualify for membership aside from passing an intellectual or doctrinal test. This is a slippery slope into a world where there

---

25. I give much credit for this section to Ray Sutton and his essay "Watery Profession," *The Geneva Papers* 3 (March 1982): 1-2.

is no arguing about someone's personal experience that is not allowed to be checked by visible evidence. Some denominations would accept experiences such as the gift of tongues to evidence the faith needed for incorporation into the church. No matter the particular measure, in the category of experiential standards faith is an acceptable testimony of a particular experience.

The biblical alternative to both is stated well by Sutton: "A person comes to baptism to *exercise* faith. When taken this way he immediately encounters an objective standard, and faith is cast into a different light. It is measured by objective obedience. As far as the church is concerned, it is not so much what one knows or experiences, but what he does."[26] Objective obedience is based on God's standard. "God expects us to measure reality by means of His covenant document, the Bible. It contains the terms of the church's treaty with God. Thus, it can be said that reality is defined covenantally."[27] Whether it be a professing adult or a child who has been consigned through the confession of his covenant head, that person is to be counted among the saved at the point at which he places himself under the terms of the covenant. He is to remain in that covenant community until he provides evidence that is contrary to his profession. In regards to those (most notably infants) consigned to the church by their head, listen again to Sutton:

> As time passes and his watery profession is denied by objective
> disobedience, then he must be disciplined back to God or out

26. Sutton, "Watery Profession," 2.
27. Sutton, "Watery Profession," 2.

of the church.... The gospel is sovereignly applied to the infant, and as he grows up he is to be told that he received the gospel at that time. It is only if he rejects the gospel later on, and apostatizes, that he is to be considered an unbeliever. If a grandfather bestows a gold coin on his grandson at birth, that gold coin is the real possession of the grandson; he does not go through a separate act of receiving the coin at some later time. He received it as a baby. So it is with baptism. God bestows it, and the infant receives it. All he has to do from that point on is to be informed about it, and to cling to it all the days of his life.[28]

We can now see clearly the indispensable role of church discipline. The function of this discipline is to protect those in the covenant community and to make way for sanctification in their lives. It is also to remove some from the fellowship should there be sufficient evidence of their apostate status. This guards the flock and preserves the purity of the church.

This raises a number of questions: "How is this to be done? Are not all sinful and living in a manner contrary to Scripture? How can anyone play God in the lives of others to the point of excommunication?" All are sinful. Repentance followed by repentant behavior is followed by acceptance by the church and by God. Absence of church government necessarily results in a church that will lose its distinct status in the world.

This is where the doctrine of representation again comes to the forefront. The church has a head who is Christ. On earth He entrusts church ministers or elders to represent Him to the

28. Sutton, "Watery Profession," 2.

church and the church to Him. Representation is governing according to the will of the head. The Head of the church has perfect judgment and His church is completely pure, consisting of the elect of God. The judgments of men are imperfect but are to reflect the perfect will of God inasmuch as they can do so this side of eternity. As the church continues to mature throughout history (for she surely has), she will more accurately reflect the will of Christ. The rolls of the church are quite literally to reflect the very rolls of heaven.

On this the credo-baptist and paedo-baptist can agree. The emphasis in this section is on the question of means and not the end. How do the church rolls in history best reflect the roll of true Israel in heaven? In far too many instances the church has answered this question in terms of rational or experiential evidence rather than the evidence of objective obedience measured against the Word of God. Reason and experience are certainly used in measuring objective obedience but they are not the standard themselves.

I contend that the absence of church discipline in our day has created much confusion over baptism and the nature of church membership. The question of retaining membership in the church is generally not dealt with at all. Yet, it is fundamental not only to preserving the church but to giving the church its very definition. The church on earth in history should be confined to those that confess Christ and place themselves and all those under their authority under His Lordship. These as well as their functional subordinates must continue to reflect this Lordship.

With regard to infants and baptism, Paul Jewett is wrong when he says, speaking of paedo-baptists, "The times have changed, but the theology is the same. The children of the saints are holy by natural pedigree, not by personal experience."[29] It is neither. These children are holy (set apart) by covenant. And within the context of Christ-like governance in the church these children will either evidence the work of the Holy Spirit in their lives over time or they will not. It is incumbent upon those ministering in the name of Christ to protect and discipline them according to the terms of the covenant under which they were placed.[30]

CONCLUSION

The structure of the covenant family unit has not changed with the coming of Christ. God is still God of the family and is represented through a covenant head with functional subordinates. In the New Testament it is clear that the intended head is the husband with a wife that supports and helps govern the household according to the Word of God. This family works to evangelize and teach first their household members and also the community and world around them. There is also continuity in Scripture in how the family structure and the covenant people of God

---

29. Paul K. Jewett, *Infant Baptism and the Covenant of Grace: An Appraisal of the Argument That as Infants Were Once Circumcised, so They Should Now Be Baptized* (Grand Rapids: Eerdmans, 1978), 125.

30. Gregg Strawbridge has provided a good outline demonstrating the inclusion of children among the covenant people throughout both the Old and New Testaments. (*Covenantal Infant Baptism: An Outlined Defense* [Brownston, PA: WordMP3, 1998].)

interact. In the Old Testament, household members could be consigned to the people of God through the head. All evidence in the New Testament points to continuity in this respect.

New Testament baptism pictures the work of Christ and incorporates a person into the church. It is no mere symbol that publicly identifies one with the church. Neither is it a mystical union with Christ ensuring the election of the individual. It is a covenant union that pictures a formal placement of the individual under the terms of God's Word and His delegated authority in the church. "[B]aptism is to be more comprehensively understood as a sealing with the name of the Trinity invoked in the consecration oath in recognition that the triune Lord is God of the covenant oath and its dual sanctions."[31] The church authority serves, protects, and disciplines the covenant community and in doing so keeps the church pure. In judging according to Scripture, those in authority work to keep their rolls as a dim reflection of the very rolls of heaven.

Infants of confessing heads are baptized and consigned to the church because they are within the authority sphere of that head. Their confession is made for them by the one who represents them. This is precisely what we continue to see in the New Testament when households are baptized.

> These are the facts about those baptized. From this we learn that of the *nine people* singled-out in the baptism narratives— *five had their households baptized* (Cornelius, the Jailer, Lydia, Crispus [inferred], Stephanas), two had no household for ob-

---

31. Kline, *By Oath Consigned*, 80.

vious reasons (eunuch & Paul). That leaves Simon, who actually turned out to be an unbeliever, and Gaius, whom Paul
baptized (1 Cor. 1:14). As for Simon, I think it is reasonable to
conclude that he was an *atypical case*. Certainly his case would
be a less than ideal basis for the Baptist view, since he turned
out to be an unbeliever. As for Gaius, in Romans 16:23 we
read that "Gaius [is] host to me and to the whole church."
This implies he was a man of some means. As such, he may
have had at least household servants, if not a familial household. Gaius is mentioned with Crispus, who was a household
head. Crispus "believed in the Lord with all his household
(Acts 18:8)." Thus, the household was undoubtedly baptized
with him. Yet Paul said in no uncertain terms, "I baptized *none
of you* except Crispus and Gaius" (1 Cor. 1:14). Paul could
name Crispus as head of the baptized household, just as he
could have with Gaius. As would be perfectly intelligible to any
first century Jew, it seems that Paul simply spoke of Crispus as
representing the household in the administration of baptism.
Therefore, if Gaius had a household, it is quite reasonable to
believe that it was baptized, just like Crispus' household.[32]

The onus is on a credobaptist to explain away all of the evidence in favor of a continuing covenant structure in the New
Testament. Baptism marks out God's people from the world and
"... the parental authority of the confessors of the covenant faith
defines the bounds of the covenant community.... Those under

---

32. Gregg Strawbridge, *Baptism in the Bible and Infant Baptism* (Brownstown, PA:
WordMP3, 2006), 6, italics and brackets in original.

that parental authority are to be consigned to the Lord by the appointed sign of incorporation into the covenant congregation."[33]

God chooses to relate to His creation through a covenant structure as previously defined. If we understand and accept how heaven and earth interact on this point, we avoid two major errors in relating to God. One is the error of resigning ourselves to a solely material world in which there is no room for a God at all. The other is tending toward a mystical union with God in which there is no time and space element or an unpredictable one. Without legal covenant boundaries we lose any real sense of cause and effect in history. In addition, the boundaries marking the people of God become invisible. In essence, the Baptist begins to walk down what starts to feel like a very Gnostic road.

So, understanding the importance of the covenant concept and rightly determining the bounds of the covenant, one can understand the significance of baptism. Baptism is a picture of the very work of Christ among men. It is a sign of both His cleansing work in the life of a believer and His judgment in the life of one who would reject Him. It marks out the people of God in history. In the eyes of God, children of confessors begin their lives as they always have: they are incorporated into His people the church. I close with a quote from Kline:

> For those who are baptized according to the secondary principle of authority as well as for those who are baptized according to the primary principle of confession, baptism is a sign of incorpo-

33. Kline, *Kingdom Prologue*, 362.

ration within the judicial sphere of Christ's covenant lordship for a final verdict of blessing or curse. In the one case the reception of baptism is a matter of active commitment; in the other, of passive consecration. But in every instance, to be baptized is to be consigned by oath to the Lord of redemptive judgment.[34]

34. Kline, *By Oath Consigned*, 102.

CHAPTER 5:
NEW COVENANT TEXTS REVISITED

HAVING WORKED THROUGH THE UNDER-standing of what constitutes (defines) a covenant, covenant institutions, and their application to baptism and the church, a curious question arises. From a scriptural standpoint (over and against a historical argument), how could someone not maintain a paedo-baptist perspective? I believe the answer to this question centers around two primary texts in Scripture. Without the confusion over these two passages, I believe the debate over infant baptism would have been over centuries ago. These are the well-known New Covenant passages in the books of Jeremiah and Hebrews.

These texts are cited as primary support for the idea that those within the New Covenant administration are comprised only of God's elect. That is, they have before the world's foundations been chosen as one of God's people in eternity. Their sins have been atoned for and their eternal salvation is secure.

It follows that if this is the case, and baptism is the sign of the New Covenant, then children of believers cannot be baptized as they would be receiving the sign prior to any confession of Christ as their Savior and Lord (even though this does not equate with election). Hence, this understanding of the New Covenant determines one's conclusion on infant baptism. *A person's doctrine of the covenant will ultimately determine their view on baptism.*

So what are we to make of these texts? Are God's New Covenant people in history comprised of only God's elect? To answer these questions, we will need to look in detail at the passages as well as the historical context of the time when Hebrews was composed. At the same time, a backdrop of the previous chapters will have to be kept in mind in regards to covenant structure.

HISTORICAL CONTEXT OF THE BOOK OF HEBREWS

As with any book in the Holy Scripture, the audience and historical context of the writing is vitally important. This is especially true in the book of Hebrews since the contemporary context was a unique, transitional time in the early life of the church. The book of Hebrews was written to a Jewish Christian audience. "The social and religious roots of this community are almost certainly to be traced to the Jewish quarters and to participation in the life of a Hellenistic synagogue."[1] They were also an early Christian assembly and as such were living in a time of persecution and difficulty. Their participation in and among Jewish life, as well as the presence of persecution, presented a temptation:

> The targeted audience was an assembly in crisis. There had been defections from their number (10:25). Among those who remained, there was a loss of confidence in the viability of their convictions. They displayed lack of interest in the message of salvation they had embraced (2:1-4), which formerly had given them a sense of identity as the new covenant people of God.... One consideration that alarmed the writer was the group's attraction for traditions that he regarded as conflicting with the word of God preached by their former leaders.[2]

The Old Covenant traditions referred to above were surrounding the Jewish Christians in a time following the ascension of Christ but prior to the destruction of the temple. These Christians had not heard the testimony of Christ directly from Him; they were one generation removed. In addition to this there was a number of Jewish sects operating around them: Herodians with their Jewish political presence; the upper-class

1. William L. Lane, *Hebrews: Word Biblical Commentary*, 2 vols. (Dallas, TX: Word, 1991), 1:liv.
2. Lane, 1:lxi.

Sadducees; the ascetic Essenes; the Pharisees who wanted to bring back old Israel; even the zealous Maccabees. They all espoused doctrines and rites of Israel which rejected Christ, and all were still looking toward political salvation.

With this in mind, this once-removed generation was susceptible to believing that Christ was truly dead and gone and perhaps believed that they were all wrong in their new-found faith. At best it could have been a point of major confusion. This is the group to whom the author of Hebrews is writing, and that is why the message is so important! "[T]he whole practical thrust of the epistle is to persuade those to whom it is addressed to resist the strong temptation to seek an easing of the hardships attendant on their Christian confession by accommodating it to the regime of the former covenant...."[3]

Hence, there is in the book one overarching theme of the supremacy of Christ over and against the Levitical priesthood and the entire ceremonial nature of the Old Covenant administration. The audience of the letter was quite literally in danger of compromising and trampling the work of Christ for the sake of adhering to the doctrine and rituals of the Old Covenant era. They had already become less attentive to the instruction of the church (5:11–14), and some had quit meeting regularly altogether (10:25).

This early church community needed a word from God to help them cling to the message of the gospel during trying and confusing times. They were privileged in their position in Christ,

3. Philip Edgcumbe Hughes, A Commentary on the Epistle to the Hebrews (Grand Rapids: Eerdmans, 1977), 10.

and the author of Hebrews intends to drive home the supremacy of Christ and the corresponding promises of the New Covenant administration that are not only better but everlasting.

It is also important to understand that, as in most of the epistles of the New Testament, the book of Hebrews is written to a community of believers, covenantally bound in their confession of Christ. They do indeed have functional subordination or hierarchy, laws, and discipline. Whereas the text has application to individuals, the message is to a covenanted community of believers. This is key to understanding chapters 8–10, just as certainly as it is key to understanding the whole letter. If the quotes from Jeremiah are not read in terms of covenant structure, representation, or the "one and the many," they will be dangerously individualized, upsetting the intents of the passage.

The focus in the passage is God's relationship to His people. Lane comments on chapter 8:

> The relationship between God and his people, which was the intention of the covenant concluded at Sinai but which was broken by the past failure of Israel to observe the conditions of the relationship established by God (v9), will be restored. Redemptive grace reaches its zenith in the full and final realization of this promise through Christ. The inauguration of the new covenant with the entrance of the eschatological high priest into the heavenly sanctuary (v6) indicates the privileged status of the Christian community.[4]

4. Lane, *Hebrews*, 209-210.

Paul Ellingworth, in his *New International Greek Testament Commentary on Hebrews*, notes,

> Even in Jeremiah, however, the new covenant is still with a people, "the house of Israel and...the house of Judah"; so even more strongly Joel 2:28-32 = Acts 2:17-21, "all flesh"; identified immediately, however, as "your sons and your daughters." In Hebrews, which (unlike 1 Pet. 2:5) does not describe believers as a priesthood, the author's immediate concern is with the work of Christ. When he finally turns, in 10:19ff., to its significance for believers, it is for believers as a group....[5]

Having covered the historical setting and touching on the covenantal nature of the message and intended audience, we can now look briefly at the specific "New Covenant" text from Jeremiah 31 quoted in Hebrews 8.

> Behold, the days are coming, declares the Lord,
> when I will establish a new covenant with the house of Israel
> and with the house of Judah,
> not like the covenant that I made with their fathers
> on the day when I took them by the hand to bring them out
> of the land of Egypt.
> For they did not continue in my covenant,
> and so I showed no concern for them, declares the Lord.
> For this is the covenant that I will make with the house of Israel

5. Paul Ellingworth, *The Epistle to the Hebrews: New International Greek Testament Commentary* (Grand Rapids: Eerdmans, 1993), 414.

after those days, declares the Lord:

I will put my laws into their minds,

and write them on their hearts,

and I will be their God,

and they shall be my people.

And they shall not teach, each one his neighbor

and each one his brother, saying, 'Know the Lord,'

for they shall all know me,

from the least of them to the greatest.

For I will be merciful toward their iniquities,

and I will remember their sins no more. (Heb. 8:8-12)

* * * * *

[N]ot like the covenant I made with their fathers on the day
when I took them by the hand to bring them out of the land
of Egypt. For they did not continue in my covenant, and so I
showed no concern for them, declares the Lord. (Heb. 8:9a;
Jer. 31:32)

Jeremiah 31:32 states, "my covenant which they broke." Who
is "they" in the text? It is the covenant community of Israel.
It could not relate directly to individuals. Moses is featured
in the Hebrews 11 "hall of faith." Joshua and Caleb did not
individually break covenant, nor can we deem them unsaved
as such. The text shows that comparisons between the Old
and New Covenants do not primarily focus on individuals.
Some in the wilderness did not fall away and some in the New

Testament are excommunicated (or fall away), as is clear with the sexually immoral man in 1 Corinthians 5:

> It is actually reported that there is sexual immorality among you, and of a kind that is not tolerated even among pagans, for a man has his father's wife. And you are arrogant! Ought you not rather to mourn? Let him who has done this be removed from among you.
>
> For though absent in body, I am present in spirit; and as if present, I have already pronounced judgment on the one who did such a thing. When you are assembled in the name of the Lord Jesus and my spirit is present, with the power of our Lord Jesus, you are to deliver this man to Satan for the destruction of the flesh, so that his spirit may be saved in the day of the Lord. (vv. 1-5)

The New Covenant with God's people will continue, although some will fall away from the covenant. The Old Covenant was "broken" but not all individuals in the Old Covenant were damned. The structure of both covenants is the same. "The last two lines of v. 10 present the new covenant as identical in form with the old (cf. Ex. 6:7; Lv. 26:12; Dt. 26:17-19; Ezk. 37:27); only the spirit is different."[6] This is consistent with Jeremiah when he says in 32:40, "that they may not turn from me." Again, this is the people as a whole, not just individuals who had broken faith. It is an everlasting covenant (32:40) and hence will not have the same fate as the old one. There will be

6. Ellingworth, 417.

no other bride in the future for Jesus Christ. His bride now is the church and we have been assured of a marriage with no divorce. Israel "did not continue" in His covenant. The New Covenant body of believers as the covenant community will.

> I will put my laws into their minds, and write them on their hearts. (Heb. 8:10b; cf. 10:16; Jer. 31:33b)

The intended contrast here must not be missed. The writer is contrasting the Old Covenant (the laws being written on tablets of stone) with the New Covenant (the laws being written on the hearts of His people through the coming of the Holy Spirit at Pentecost). This contrast is consistent with the theme of this section. In the previous arrangement with Israel, the high priesthood mediated between the people and the presence of God. This presence was typified through the ark which contained the law of God written on stone tablets. In the New Covenant arrangement we have a new High Priest who is Christ.

As the writer of Hebrews seeks to drive home many times, this is the true presence of God as we approach Mount Zion (chapter 12) and there is no longer a curtain dividing us, mediated through an inferior priesthood and the blood of goats and bulls, which cannot take away sins (10:4). The laws which represent the unchanging character of God are not housed in the ark of the (old) covenant but have been given through the Holy Spirit at Pentecost. The contrast drives home the superior power available to the church over and above that of Israel.

In addition to this contrast being consistent with the overall theme and message of the book, it is also apparent when
looking at texts such as Deuteronomy 30:14: "But the word is
very near you. It is in your mouth and in your heart, so that
you can do it." If we individualize the passage from Jeremiah,
we must also do so with this verse. But we are unable to do
so, understanding from above that "they" broke the covenant.
The primary context of the passage is not in reference to some
salvific nature of the New Covenant. It is a contrast of the
Holy Spirit's power and presence over and above the Old
Covenant. This is the definitive newness of the covenant. The
structure is not.

> I will be their God, and they shall be my people (Heb. 8:10c;
> Jer. 31:33c)

Unlike above, this is not a contrast to the relationship God
had with His bride Israel. It actually puts the church on the
same footing with Israel. The church is His New Covenant
bride and the verse is surrounded by a context that elevates not
the structure or legal relationship, but the superiority of promises and sacrifice. The same promise was given to Abraham
and Moses to be "God to you and your descendants":

> And I will establish my covenant between me and you and
> your offspring after you throughout their generations for an
> everlasting covenant, to be God to you and to your offspring
> after you. (Gen. 17:7)

I will dwell among the people of Israel and will be their God.
(Exod. 29:45)

... that he may establish you today as his people, and that he
may be your God, as he promised you, and as he swore to your
fathers, to Abraham, to Isaac, and to Jacob. (Deut. 29:13)

Again, the understanding that the covenant is made with a
people is driven home. Ultimately in heaven, this eschatological people will be the elect of God. In the meantime, God is
using two covenant administrations in history to bring about
His ultimate purpose of redemption to the world. Another way
to say it would be that there are two Israels in history but only
one true Israel that will prove faithful, as Abraham's true descendants are in fact followers of Christ that truly believe and
therefore persevere. He alone looks into the hearts of man.

[T]hey shall not teach each one his neighbor and each one his
brother, saying, "Know the Lord," for they shall all know me,
from the least of them to the greatest. (Heb 8:11; Jer. 31:34a)

Without understanding the larger context of Scripture, this
verse may seem somewhat confusing. Would this mean that
individuals within the New Covenant would not teach each
other as they would all be elect in Christ? How could this really
make sense within the context of operating on earth where we
cannot fully discern the hearts of men?

One question to give insight might be, what kind of teaching existed in the Old Testament that would not be in the New? It could not be the teaching that occurs within the ministry of the church.

> It refers to something that was part of the ceremonial legislation of the old covenant that is going to cease, will no longer be practiced, and will be removed in the new covenant. Second, teaching is involved. The passage addresses something with regard to the spreading of the knowledge of the Lord that previously occurred among the covenant people of God.[7]

Again, one of the central thrusts of the overall context of the letter is the doing away of the ceremonial law practices. The knowledge and practice of the laws resided with the Levitical priesthood; they were central to teaching God's people Israel and representing the knowledge of the Lord to them.[8] In the first part of this verse Jeremiah was pointing out that this would cease. This is a message that needed to be heard by that early Christian community as they saw these practices continue to surround them with the presence of the temple.

The second phrase, "from the least of them to the greatest," needs only to be interpreted in light of how the phrase is used in the rest of Jeremiah:

7. Jeffrey D. Niell, "The Newness of the New Covenant," in *The Case for Covenantal Infant Baptism*, 146-147.
8. Niell, 153.

The Hebrew phrase that is translated "least...greatest" (sometimes rendered "great and small") is used seven times in Jeremiah, and each time it refers to classes or ranks of persons. When referring to the least and the greatest, he is consistently referring to all classes of people (6:13, 8:10, 16:6, 31:34, 41:1, 44:12).[9]

The Levitical priests were a special class of people whose role and function under the Old Covenant was to be done away with. There would no longer be a special class possessing the knowledge of the Lord. All classes of people would be privy to it and would engage the throne room of God directly through their new High Priest from the line of Melchizedek, Jesus Christ.

As for these phrases applying to the individual, Gregg Strawbridge provides keen insight:

[T]o absolutize the prophetic words like, "they shall all know Me, from the least of them to the greatest of them" is untenable. (In the first place this overlooks Jeremiah's own use of the phrase "least to greatest.") The "New Covenant Objection" really arises from the exegetical error of absolutizing such prophetic language, coupled with an inadequate Biblical theology of covenants. Neither the writer of Hebrews, nor any other New Testament writer interprets Jeremiah to mean that only regenerate individuals are covenanted with. Prophetic language often is hyperbolic and care must be taken when it is read in a quantitatively literal fashion. For example, God

9. Niell, 152.

called "all the families of the kingdoms of the north...and they
will come, and they will set each one his throne at the entrance
of the gates of Jerusalem, and against all its walls round about,
and against all the cities of Judah" (Jer. 1:15). Read in a quantitatively absolute fashion, this would have been a physical im-
possibility. As has been adequately demonstrated, this was not
Hebrews' purpose in the text cited and is inconsistent with the
entire theme and refrain of the book.[10]

One of the central "themes and refrains" of Hebrews is that of
possible apostasy from the New Covenant. Constant warnings
of this are provided throughout the book of Hebrews (3:6-4:7;
6:4-6; 10:26-31; 12:14-17, 25-29). They are warned so as not
to end up like the man in 1 Corinthians 5 above.

Hebrews is an odd book to cite for support of the idea that
the New Covenant is only comprised of the elect. The warnings
in Hebrews are also consistent with other passages in the New
Testament (John 15; Rom. 11:20-22; 2 Pet. 1:9-11; Jude 12).
As a covenant member, Judas took part in the New Covenant
meal and apostatized. He was not elect (Luke 22:3), but he was
a professing follower of Jesus Christ who participated in the
fellowship meal with Jesus. An understanding of the possibility of apostasy in the life of New Covenant members not only
gives insight to the many New Testament passages cited above
but it lends needed insight into the passage in Hebrews 6:

10. Gregg Strawbridge, "Appendix B: A Brief Exposition of Jeremiah 31:31-34,"
in *Covenantal Infant Baptism: An Outlined Defense*.

For it is impossible, in the case of those who have once been enlightened, who have tasted the heavenly gift, and have shared in the Holy Spirit, and have tasted the goodness of the word of God and the powers of the age to come, and then have fallen away, to restore them again to repentance, since they are crucifying once again the Son of God to their own harm and holding him up to contempt. For land that has drunk the rain that often falls on it, and produces a crop useful to those for whose sake it is cultivated, receives a blessing from God. But if it bears thorns and thistles, it is worthless and near to being cursed, and its end is to be burned. (vv. 4-8)

It is a blessing to live life within the boundaries of the set-apart people of God. We are privy to the teaching and preaching of the Word of God, the fellowship of believers, the fellowship with Christ through the sacrament of the Lord's Supper and the discipline and watchful care of able shepherds. We see this same structure and response of God to a holy and privileged bride, Israel:

And you, Capernaum, will you be exalted to heaven? You will be brought down to Hades. For if the mighty works done in you had been done in Sodom, it would have remained until this day. But I tell you that it will be more tolerable on the day of judgment for the land of Sodom than for you. (Matt. 11:23-24)

All are judged under the covenant at creation but God's people as His bride have always been judged more severely. It is understandable that this would not be a comfortable doctrine, but it cannot be dismissed. The church is privileged as the bride of Christ. Part of the privilege is an abolition of the special class of Levites. From the least to the greatest, we can all approach Mount Zion and the heavenly throneroom with confidence. The New Covenant administration through the church will help mature God's people and bring about His redemptive purposes in this world. The famed already/not-yet tension is present in this passage even outside a good understanding of the discussion above.

> We look forward to the day when the New Covenant itself comes to a glorious maturity—and the bride will have no spot or wrinkle, and we will all know the Lord. The New Covenant will bring a much greater outpouring of efficacious glory from God than was previously seen in the world.... The Levitical administration was for Israel in a condition of immaturity; it was entirely inadequate for the harvest of all nations.[11]

> For I will be merciful toward their iniquities, and I will remember their sins no more. (Heb. 8:12; Jer. 31:34b)

Is this new in the New Covenant? It cannot be. God fully atoned for the sin of His elect saints in the Old Testament just as He does in the New. Justification by faith has always been a reality as Hebrews 11 points out. Pardoning sin is not something new that is restricted to members of the New Covenant, so this verse

11. Wilson, 37.

cannot refer to a distinctive of the New Covenant being comprised of only elect members whose sin is atoned for.

One might say then, "Of course sins were atoned for in the heart of those saved by faith in the Old Testament; but that is the difference. In the New Covenant, all members have faith and are therefore elect. Their sins are remembered no more." One Baptist has put it, "In the context of Jer. 31:34 for God 'not to remember' means that no action will need to be taken in the new age against sin. In the end, to be under the terms of this covenant entails that one experiences a full and complete salvation."[12]

This is all fine and well but it divorces the concept of remembering sins no more from the context of the book. Again, the focus is on the inferiority of the ceremonial law system and of the priesthood. "The inadequacy of the cultus was not due to its being a sacrificial system. It was due to its sacrificial system being imperfect."[13] The whole point is that sacrifices in the Old Covenant did not take away sin. Christ's ultimate sacrifice did. The Old Covenant people lived in a world where the atonement for their sin was ritually and continually pointed to in the sacrifices. There was to come a time when these continual sacrifices were to cease.

> Thus it was necessary for the copies of the heavenly things to
> be purified with these rites, but the heavenly things themselves
> with better sacrifices than these. For Christ has entered, not

12. Wellum, 146.
13. Ellingworth, 411.

into holy places made with hands, which are copies of the true things, but into heaven itself, now to appear in the presence of God on our behalf. Nor was it to offer himself repeatedly, as the high priest enters the holy places every year with blood not his own, for then he would have had to suffer repeatedly since the foundation of the world. But as it is, he has appeared once for all at the end of the ages to put away sin by the sacrifice of himself. (Heb. 9:23-26)

With the death and resurrection of Christ, the sins of His people were atoned for once and for all. The writer says in Hebrews 10:17-18, "[T]hen he adds, I will remember their sins and their lawless deeds no more. Where there is forgiveness of these, there is no longer any offering for sin." We see again the intent to drive home the assurance of there being no need for the continual sacrifices of Israel's priests. These are a people in the original context of Jeremiah who were to be exiled and to have their temple destroyed.

From a New Testament perspective and application they are back in the land and there is a rebuilt temple. There was a looming question in their minds as Jews continued sacrificial practices around them. The question was, "Are we truly forgiven?" In the letter to them they hear consolation. Their sins are truly forgiven through the sacrifice of Jesus Christ.

The point was that there were no longer any sacrifices needed. There is still, though, an earthly people and ministry of the church. No one can fully discern whose sin has truly been atoned for through the death of Christ, but we can work within the covenant structure of the church by taking men at their confession and working within the context of church discipline. The structure is designed to work for the purification of the people over time, further reflecting the rolls of heaven and the one day in which all saints will be gathered before the throne.

CONCLUSION

The New Covenant texts of Jeremiah and Hebrews are a glorious declaration of the sufficiency of Christ. This new Christian assembly in crisis needed a reminder of first principles of the faith. They needed to be reminded that Jesus' sacrifice was truly sufficient. They needed to be warned not to fall away. This was the baptized community of Christ in covenant. It was the New Covenant. This New Covenant had at its foundation the blood of the true sacrifice and the power of the Holy Spirit. To take the texts to mean that God's covenant structure was to be done away with and that God's people on earth are only the invisible or eschatological elect at best divorces them from the overall context of the book of Hebrews. At worst it tends toward a Gnostic division of heaven and earth.

It is no wonder the issue of infant baptism becomes distorted with this understanding of the covenant. Listen to Jewett:

> The covenantees are not those who are *born* into the covenant, those whose father and mother have the law "written upon their hearts," but those who *themselves* have had this experience, having been born again by the Spirit of God. This sub-

jective, inward, existential, spiritual change is the hallmark of the new covenant.[14]

This statement misunderstands the relationship between the family and church covenants which has been discussed. Additionally, it tends almost to an other-worldly covenant that cannot be perceived or interacted with on earth. The church on earth is relegated to a contractual institution at best in which members gather but are not called out or set apart by covenant. The material world is done away with and a discussion of the New Covenant relates only to another more fully "spiritual" world. Listen again to an extended quotation from Strawbridge:

> It is true that mere natural descent is insufficient to guarantee the fullest reception of the covenant promised blessings. This being true during the Old Testament, according to Paul, then how does this truth affect the question of the sign of covenant given to believers' children? In the previous eras they received it, though it was still true that all who were authorized by God to receive the sign did not partake of the reality signified. The argument is fatally flawed. It says that since only the truly spiritual seed received the promises, then only the spiritual seed have a right to the sign. But this argument (from Paul's statements about true Israel) is fallacious. Because, it is simply not true nor intended by God's command that only the true "spiritual seed" (the elect) are to receive the sign of the covenant. The sign is a visible sign, for visible members of God's people.

14. Jewett, 228, italics in original.

It is not enough to prove that only the elect are elected. This is granted. God, who knew about Esau, still commanded the sign of circumcision on him, even though he did not have a circumcised heart. What must be proved if the argument for covenant inclusion, leading to infant baptism is to be dismissed, is not the truth of election—but that only those that are elect are to receive the sign of the covenant. It is certainly impossible to prove this was God's intention in the Old Testament and it is just as impossible in the new covenant.... Consider the case in point further, Esau. Not denying the truth of election, the writer of Hebrews indicates that Esau was a covenant breaker, "See to it that no one comes short of the grace of God...that there be no immoral or godless person like Esau, who sold his own birthright for a single meal" (Heb. 12:15-16). Thus one is still warranted in putting the sign on those of whom we do not have infallible assurance of their election.[15]

One might contend that the Old and New Covenants are different in structure and therefore what was done in regard to the application of signs in the Old Covenant is not what is done in the New. This is precisely what the rest of this book seeks to address. The way in which God relates to people on earth has not changed. He has not substituted a mystical connection with believers in the New Covenant, a connection that cannot be perceived on earth, for the legal connection that can be seen, set apart, and governed. The structure within

15. Gregg Strawbridge, "Appendix B: A Brief Exposition of Jeremiah 31:31-34," in *Covenantal Infant Baptism: An Outlined Defense.*

which God relates to His people on earth has not changed. Paul drives this home in the following passage:

> For I do not want you to be unaware, brothers, that our fathers were all under the cloud, and all passed through the sea, and all were baptized into Moses in the cloud and in the sea, and all ate the same spiritual food, and all drank the same spiritual drink. For they drank from the spiritual Rock that followed them, and the Rock was Christ. Nevertheless, with most of them God was not pleased, for they were overthrown in the wilderness. (1 Cor. 10:1-5)

Just like the New Covenant church today, Paul says they ate and drank from Christ. Nevertheless, "with most of them God was not pleased." Both covenant administrations had their root in Christ. The structure was the same. Kline says it well when he comments on the treatment of the olive tree in Romans 11:16:

> This holiness is not that inward spiritual holiness which is the fruit of the sanctifying work of the Spirit in the elect, for it is shared by those (branches) whose nonelection is betrayed by their eventually being broken off from the olive tree. Hence the olive tree as such does not represent the election but the covenant, and the holiness attributed to the tree, root and branches, is the formal status-holiness of membership in the covenant institution.[16]

---

16. Kline, *Kingdom Prologue*, 362.

He relates this directly to children of believers by saying,

> [B]y applying the covenantal blessing of the fifth command-
> ment to the children of Christian parents (Eph. 6:1-3; cf. Col.
> 3:20; Exod. 20:12) Paul indicates that they are not merely un-
> der the call to enter the covenant but are *in* the holy covenant,
> consigned under its terms of blessing or curse.[17]

God relates to His creation through covenant. This did not
change with the coming of Christ. Neither did man's inability
to discern the heart. There is a real, discernible, covenant institution that operates in history. It is not only visible but it is
governed representatively by men. One day the eschatological
church will come into full view, but for now we live and operate under the terms of God's New Covenant in history.

---

17. Kline, *Kingdom Prologue*, 363.

CHAPTER 6:
COVENANT STRUCTURE AND THE WHOLE GOSPEL

THIS CHAPTER IS NOT INTENDED TO BE AN expository defense of a particular eschatological position. It is merely to provide further direction and meaning to the previous discussions in this book. A question that necessarily arises from the first five chapters of this book is, "For what purpose?" For what purpose has God provided a covenantal framework through which to work in this world? Why does covenant structure matter? For what purpose would God ordain covenant institutions, each with their own boundaries and jurisdictions? Why would He choose to relate to us through this structure?

Well, certainly the short answer is "For His own glory." Yet, how is He glorified? Certainly one aspect would be the manifestation of His rule on earth as it exists in heaven. He has finished His definitive redemptive work on earth and is ruling from His throne in heaven:

> ...when he raised him from the dead and seated him at his right hand in the heavenly places, far above all rule and authority and power and dominion, and above every name that is named, not only in this age but also in the one to come. And he put all things under his feet and gave him as head over all things to the church, which is his body, the fullness of him who fills all in all. (Eph. 1:20–23)

> For he must reign until he has put all his enemies under his feet. (1 Cor. 15:25)

He is glorified through extending His visible rule in history over all of His creation. He does this through the power of the Holy Spirit. For what purpose has God provided His covenant structure through which to work on earth? To extend His visible rule. As discussed, this rule is not established through some mystical chain of being. It is established through legal bonds between a king and his subjects.

Think about how any king would extend his rule on earth. Think about how a conquering king would go about this task. He would first establish his authority as supreme. "All authority in heaven and on earth has been given to me" (Matt. 28:18). He would set up functional subordinates to rule under him and one another. (Think elders, husbands, masters, civil magistrates.) They would represent him to his people and them to him. What else? Basic to how this king would rule would be the very laws he intended for governing every sphere of the life of his subjects. If they were to be fully conformed to his will and his character, then he would have to put laws in place that reflected his character that could be carried out by his functional subordinates: "teaching them to observe all I have commanded you" (Matt. 28:20).

For those that followed the king's laws there would be inherent blessing. Those who did not he would have to discipline. Finally, he would have to have a provision for continuing his rule after he was gone. The extent to which this conquering king could successfully carry out these things is the extent to which he would rule his kingdom.

But God is not physically present on earth. Neither is an earthly king physically present with each of his subjects. What then is present? If not a physical presence, then what? A covenant. Christ uses His covenant and His Holy Spirit to be present with us and govern His creation. They are both basic to extending His rule and His will being "done on earth as it is in heaven."

Who will experience progressive victory over time? Those who conduct themselves in terms of God's covenant with them. Who will be able to do this over time? Those who have the Holy Spirit's power.

In chapter 2 we said, God does not work through creation magically or mystically. He works through His creation representatively. He chooses to use men to carry out His rule on earth. He does supernaturally regenerate the hearts of men and exercises sovereignty over all creation. Through regeneration He gives special power to His people, and to the extent that they are loyal subjects, they see their King's rule extended. When this happens, everyone benefits. Why? Because men are living in terms of a King's law that is right, true, and brings external blessings for obedience.

Just as the wheat and tares of Matthew 13 grow together in the same field, Christ's loyal subjects grow side by side with the weeds, both maturing and differentiating themselves over time until the final judgment. The field flourishes and the weeds are not fully judged and burned for the sake of the growth of the wheat.

Let's think about this one more time. What necessarily happens when heads are obedient and covenant institutions are governed (structured, lead, disciplined, carried out) according to the Word of God? In general, this would breed institutional success. Asked another way, is there cause and effect and does God reward covenant obedience, or do actions in reference to God's Word have random consequences in history?

I think Scripture would support the former. So why does so much of the Christian church call for obedience, preach occasionally about possible rewards this side of heaven, and not expect to see Christ's rule extended visibly on earth? Why do we expect the very failure and defeat of the church in history? Again, a complete answer to these questions goes beyond the scope of this book, but I will deal with one of the major hang-ups I see today. Let's call it "sojourner theology."

SOJOURNER THEOLOGY

What I am calling sojourner theology is a certain understanding of the concept that we are "not of this world" and that we are sojourners, or strangers and pilgrims traveling through a world not our own until a day when Jesus comes to take us to a new home. Below are a few of the specific verses in Scripture from which these concepts are derived:

> Jesus answered, "My kingdom is not of this world. If my kingdom were of this world, my servants would have been fighting, that I might not be delivered over to the Jews. But my kingdom is not from the world." (John 18:36)

> Do not love the world or the things in the world. If anyone loves the world, the love of the Father is not in him. (1 John 2:15)

> Beloved, I urge you as sojourners and exiles to abstain from the passions of the flesh, which wage war against your soul. Keep your conduct among the Gentiles honorable, so that when they speak against you as evildoers, they may see your good deeds and glorify God on the day of visitation. (1 Pet. 2:11–12)

The verses above seem to conflict with the following verses:

> And Jesus came and said to them, "All authority in heaven and on earth has been given to me. Go therefore and make disciples of all nations, baptizing them in the name of the Father and of the Son and of the Holy Spirit, teaching them to ob-

serve all that I have commanded you. And behold, I am with you always, to the end of the age." (Matt. 28:18-20)

For he must reign until he has put all his enemies under his feet. The last enemy to be destroyed is death. For "God has put all things in subjection under his feet." But when it says, "all things are put in subjection," it is plain that he is excepted who put all things in subjection under him. (1 Cor. 15:25-27)

Now is the judgment of this world; now will the ruler of this world be cast out. (John 12:31)

I have said these things to you, that in me you may have peace. In the world you will have tribulation. But take heart; I have overcome the world. (John 16:33)

The earth is the Lord's and the fullness thereof, the world and those who dwell therein (Ps. 24:1)

Which is it? Is the world something for us to revile and remain separated from? Do we just live in this world and expect only historical victory in terms of men's souls? Does God rule over the earth or just His church on earth? Does God "so love the world," but we are not supposed to love it or anything in it? Are we merely wandering as exiles on earth or do we have another purpose as we await the second coming of Christ?

First, when Jesus says His kingdom is not of this world, the words "of" or "from" are not the same as "over" or "in."

It sure seems that as the King of kings, Christ is certainly ruling over this world.

In addition, whatever its nature, His kingdom is manifested in this world. The emphasis to Pilate in the verse from John above is that Christ's power is derived from a source that transcends this world—from heaven's throne room. Satan was defeated at the cross and all authority has been given to Christ—"given" from a source not of this world. Pilate gets his authority and power from earthly sources. Christ's power comes from God Himself and is not "of" this world.

It is precisely this power which is used to establish Christ's visible rule and enact His will on earth as it is seen in heaven. God loved the world, overthrew Satan's hold on the world, and "overcame" it. In heavenly places, "far above all rule and authority and power and dominion," He is the source of our power. Such power is not of this world. Yet, "all authority in heaven and on earth" has been given to Him and by His authority and through His power we are to disciple nations, baptize them, and teach them to obey His Word. While not "of" this world, He is surely over it and has commanded us to subdue it to Him.

So what do we make of verses such as, "Do not love the world or the things in the world. If anyone loves the world, the love of the Father is not in him" (1 John 2:15)? This is a world where Satan ruled. We are tasked with subduing a world that is visibly corrupt. Jesus' words were no different than God's words in Leviticus 18:3-4: "You shall not do as they do in the land of Egypt, where you lived, and you shall not do as they do in the land of Canaan, to which I am bringing you. You shall not walk in their statutes."

God does not say this so they should separate themselves from the land of Canaan. Far from that, He says He is bringing them there. He just wants them to walk in His statues, opposed to the statues of the corrupt world that will be surrounding them.

Unconquered Canaan was evil. Of course the world is as well. The intent was not to leave it so. "And we have seen and testify that the Father has sent his Son to be the Savior of the world" (1 John 4:14). "For everyone who has been born of God overcomes the world. And this is the victory that has overcome the world—our faith. Who is it that overcomes the world except the one who believes that Jesus is the Son of God?" (1 John 5:4–5). "The whole world lies in the power of the evil one" (1 John 5:19) currently, as did Canaan. In James 4:4: "Do you not know that friendship with the world [read Canaan] is enmity with God?"

We too are not to be separate from or passively involved in this world but are to be actively involved in carrying out the Great Commission. Such a commission is more than that of rescuing souls. It is living in the world and preaching the gospel of Jesus Christ so as to see His Word being taught and obeyed among all nations.

Hopefully having set aside the first misconception, we are now left with this concept of Christians as pilgrims or sojourners in this world. Certainly a sojourner would have certain difficultly extending Christ's visible rule on earth because by definition such an individual is a wanderer or pilgrim in a land not his own. But understanding all that has been covered above, is this really the case with the Christian?

To understand this we must first understand the time in which the New Testament Christians were living. They were in a transition between "the ages" as discussed in Scripture. Both Christ, Paul, and the writer of Hebrews speak of an age which the world was in, but that changed with the coming of Christ and the destruction of the temple in AD 70 (Matt. 24; 28; 1 Cor. 10:11; Eph. 1:21; Col. 1:26; Gal. 1:4; 1 Tim. 6:17; Titus 2:12; Heb. 6:5; 9:9; 9:26). The coming of Christ ushered in a new age.

But was Paul's and Jesus' "this age" actually coming to an end when Paul wrote, or will it yet be in our future? Paul makes this clear as well, in 1 Corinthians 10. After recounting several stories from Exodus, Paul teaches, "Now these things happened to them as an example, but they were written down for our [his and his audience's] instruction, on whom the end of the ages has come" (v. 11). It is clear from this that Paul saw himself at the end of an age—an age typified by judgment upon disobedient people.

The author of Hebrews uses a very similar expression in relation to the work of Christ: "But as it is, he has appeared once for all at the end of the ages to put away sin by the sacrifice of himself" (Heb. 9:26). It is clear here that the end of that old time period arrived in conjunction with the crucifixion of Christ.

So, from the teaching of Jesus, Paul, and the author of Hebrews, we get a very clear picture of *two* primary ages: one that endured up until the time of Christ, and another that began around that same period. I believe these two periods, being hinged upon the coming and work of Christ, pertain obviously to the Old and New Covenant administrations. Indeed, this is what the author of Hebrews himself relates. He says the New Covenant makes the Old obsolete: "And what *is becoming obsolete* and growing old *is ready to vanish away*" (Heb. 8:13). Notice, the New had in fact made the Old obsolete definitively. But as he wrote, in his time, the Old was *becoming* obsolete and was *ready* to vanish away. It had not yet been completely wiped out, but it was certainly in its dying moments.[1]

It certainly was in its dying moments. In fact, the writer of Hebrews was pleading with the church to understand such a fact and to keep their eyes firmly fixed on our High Priest Jesus Christ and the certainty of His promises during a confusing and tumultuous time. In the book of Revelation we see the final act of the destruction of the temple spoken of by Christ. This was a time of extreme transition, tribulation, and persecution in the lives of professing Christians of that time period. This takes us to a better understanding of Christians as sojourners and exiles.

1. Joel McDurmon, "The Great Omission," *The American Vision* (May 6, 2011): https://www.lambsreign.com/mcdurmon/the-great-omission.

> Beloved, I urge you as sojourners and exiles to abstain from
> the passions of the flesh, which wage war against your soul.
> (1 Pet. 2:11)

This is one of those times when we need to reinforce that Scripture was written for us as God's covenant people, but that does not mean it was not written to us in any specific context. To whom was Peter writing this particular text?

He was writing to literal exiles: "To those who are elect exiles of the dispersion in Pontus, Galatia, Cappadocia, Asia, and Bithynia" (1 Pet. 1:1). "And if you call on him as Father who judges impartially according to each one's deeds, conduct yourselves with fear throughout the time of your exile" (1 Pet. 1:17). The specific audience were descendants of the Babylonian exile who had not returned. He speaks to them as exiles but also assures them of their status in Christ and their place in the "last times":

> [K]nowing that you were ransomed from the futile ways inher-
> ited from your forefathers, not with perishable things such as
> silver or gold, but with the precious blood of Christ, like that
> of a lamb without blemish or spot. He was foreknown before
> the foundation of the world but was made manifest in the last
> times for the sake of you. (1 Pet. 1:18–20)

They lived in the present evil age discussed above but looked forward to the age to come, when Jesus would come in judgment on His bride Israel and take to Himself His bride, the

church (of which they were a part). Peter is very careful to instruct these exiles to exercise good conduct so that when such
a destruction of Jerusalem arrived, the rulers would see their
good works and glorify God rather than lump them in with
the other Jews who would soon be identified with rebellion
against Rome. This is why he emphasized submission to the
emperor and to the governors (1 Pet. 2:13-14).

This text surely instructs us as present-day believers, but it
in no way should be taken as specific instruction to us in a way
that assumes we live under the same circumstances as these
first-century "exiles." Nor should we be quick to dismiss the
literal sense and quickly take up a metaphorical interpretation
that cannot be rooted in the message of Scripture as a whole.
Why let a metaphorical interpretation of 1 Peter up-end the
"conquering" aspect of Christ's Lordship in time and in history and relegate the Christian people as exiles (a theological
category for those under judgment), wandering in the desert
until Jesus' return—a return that would see victory only at that
time because somehow the Holy Spirit is impotent during the
here and now?

With the coming of Christ we "are no longer strangers and
aliens" (Eph. 2:19). Unlike the strangers and exiles prior to
the coming of Christ spoken of by Paul and also by the writer
of Hebrews in chapter 11, we have ceased wandering and have
come to the destination spoken of in Hebrews 12. It is through
our being united to the one true sacrifice and Savior of the
world that we can be assured of fulfilling His mandate—a
mandate that consists not of wandering in the wilderness and

saving souls along the way, but of the conversion of souls and seeing His rule extended throughout the nations of the earth.

THE WILDERNESS OR CANAAN?

The people of Israel were once sojourners in Canaan before God brought them into the promised land: "I also established my covenant with them to give them the land of Canaan, the land in which they lived as sojourners" (Exod. 6:4). God's Old Testament people of faith (Heb. 11) were also sojourners in a land that only their descendants (spiritual) were able to see. We now live in that land and possess the promised Christ. I believe many of the issues discussed in this chapter can be distilled into an understanding that we as Christians in the present age are not wandering in the "wilderness," but being led by Christ in subduing "Canaan."

In addition to Israel being God's Old Covenant people, they were a picture of God's New Covenant people, the church, made up of Jews and Gentiles. They were delivered out of the chains of Egypt, brought through a wilderness, and then given a land to subdue under the leadership of Joshua. We have been delivered from the bondage of our sin, brought through a wilderness, and are now being led by Jesus (Joshua) in subduing the whole earth.

Unlike Israel, we have the Holy Spirit and our trial in the wilderness was overcome through Christ's victory over Satan in the wilderness. His death, burial, and resurrection meant a definitive defeat of the evil one who had for so long maintained a grip on the world. Satan's lease expired at the cross and the whole land was turned over to Christ's adopted sons.

This was what the year of Jubilee pointed to with God's Old Testament people. During this year (every 50 years) the land in Israel would return to its original Hebrew family owners. Jesus' ministry marked the fulfillment of this principle when God returned the land back to His adopted sons. Satan's temporary lease of God's land (Ps. 24:1, "The earth is the LORD's") is up. We see this at the very beginning of Christ's ministry directly following the temptation in the wilderness.

> And he came to Nazareth, where he had been brought up. And as was his custom, he went to the synagogue on the Sabbath day, and he stood up to read. And the scroll of the prophet Isaiah was given to him. He unrolled the scroll and found the place where it was written,
>
> "The Spirit of the Lord is upon me,
> because he has anointed me
> to proclaim good news to the poor.
> He has sent me to proclaim liberty to the captives
> and recovering of sight to the blind,
> to set at liberty those who are oppressed,
> to proclaim the year of the Lord's favor."
>
> And he rolled up the scroll and gave it back to the attendant and sat down. And the eyes of all in the synagogue were fixed on him. And he began to say to them, "Today this Scripture has been fulfilled in your hearing." (Luke 4:16-21)

The Scripture from Isaiah referenced very directly the year of Jubilee. As van der Waal puts it, "The land-promise is realized by Jesus Christ. His kingship encompasses the whole earth. Although at present we do not yet see all things in subjection under Him (Heb. 2:8), still the promise remains that one day nothing will be left outside His control. We are approaching the restitution of all things."[2]

The land-promise realized was much like the typological promise given to the people of Israel in regards to Canaan. The land was not turned over as fully subject to Him. Like Canaan, we are given a world fraught with sin and are expected to be strong and courageous and exercise responsibility under God's law so that we can experience progressive victory and extend Christ's rule. To be wandering in the wilderness like Israel before entering the land would be "as if the spies sent by Israel into Canaan had been instructed to find people like Rahab, in order to convince them to leave their homes and to come to dwell in the wilderness with Israel, until the day of final judgment."[3]

Sojourner theology denies the power of the Holy Spirit in the lives of God's people and gives the church the appearance of being fearful of giants in the land. Why can they not be conquered? Because God does not intend it prior to His return? This is an abridged gospel. It destines us to wander in the wilderness until Christ's coming. This denies the intention

---

2. Van der Der Waal, 174.

3. Gary North, *Unconditional Surrender: God's Program for Victory* (Tyler, TX: Institute for Christian Economics, 1988), 210.

of covenant structure linking heaven and earth. The new "Joshua" need not be physically present in the world. Power through the Holy Spirit has been given to the church. This power is harnessed within the proper application of the covenant. The fulfillment of the land-promise discussed above is the manifestation of the original mandate in Genesis and the task of the Great Commission. Either the Holy Spirit provides what is needed to carry this out or He is impotent in the life of Christians in every area except one of limited personal piety and Sunday worship with the saints. I believe the former and regard the latter as denying fundamental ways in which men relate to one another and the world around them.

As men are changed individually to be like Christ they make decisions differently. These decisions are not limited but complete in scope. They may not make decisions consistent with their conversion, but if consistent, these decisions and the decisions of those around them who conform to God's standard (wheat or tares) shape all of life around them. We are back to a visible extension of Christ's rule.

This is a representative view of the kingdom of God. Progressively in history Christ works representatively through His people to establish His rule over every area of His creation. Then, in a final judgment at His second coming at the end of time He ushers in eternity. What was accomplished definitively at the cross is being manifested progressively in history and will one day be finally complete. This representative view helps us to understand better our citizenship in heaven and how it relates to earth. In all of this discussion perhaps you are still protesting, "But we are citizens of heaven!" Of course we are, as Paul makes very clear: "So then you are no longer strangers and aliens, but you are fellow citizens with the saints and members of the household of God" (Eph. 2:19). Does this mean our heavenly citizenship negates or renders insignificant our citizenship here on earth? Of course not. This is a false dichotomy.

But never forget: we are citizens of earth, too. We are not of the world, but we are *in* the world. We are citizens on earth. More to the point, *the whole concept of earthly political citizenship is based on the Bible's concept of supernatural citizenship.* Heavenly citizenship is the God-required model. God did not invent the category of heavenly citizenship based on the earthly model of citizenship. He did not look to Greece, Rome, or the United States Constitution to discover the proper concept of citizenship to establish in heaven....

There can be no religiously neutral society in history. There can be no religiously neutral nation. Nations, like people, are either covenant-breakers or covenant-keepers, as Sodom and Gomorrah learned too late. There can be no people who hold citizenship papers in only one nation, earth. In history, we all hold earthly citizenship papers and supernatural citizenship papers, heaven or hell.

Covenant-keepers are required by God to seek to extend God's kingdom principles on earth: the Great Commission (Matthew 28:18-20). Covenant-breakers are required by Satan to extend anti-Christian, satanic kingdom principles on earth. Thus, earth's nations in history reflect either heaven or hell on earth.[4]

Clearly we have citizenship or a commonwealth in heaven (Phil. 3:20). Yet, we are called to carry the whole gospel of Jesus Christ to the whole world in which earthly or historical citizenship is a reality. The apostle Paul appealed to his rights as a Roman citizen in his confrontation with Rome (Acts 22:25-29). He even appealed to Caesar (25:11). As the world is evangelized and names are added to the roll in heaven, and the Word of God is diligently taught, the world in which we live necessarily changes. It will visibly change through God's ordained covenant institutions.

We now run headlong into this question: whose laws are more productive in society? Do people prosper long term through obedience to humanistic law? The Bible says that the meek before God will inherit the earth—how does this happen? It happens covenantally through God's ordained institutions of the family, church, and state.

CONCLUSION

This chapter was not intended fully to explain or defend an eschatology of victory. There are volumes of books and articles that can aid in that task for the interested reader. It is merely aimed at pointing out consistency and purpose in covenant

4. Gary North, *Healer of the Nations: Biblical Blueprints for International Relations* (Ft. Worth, TX: Dominion, 1987), 142, italics in original. Also see Gary DeMar, *God and Government: A Biblical, Historical, and Constitutional Perspective* (Powder Springs, GA: American Vision, 2011).

thinking. It discussed the logical end of God's successful use of covenant structure. In this structure clear boundaries matter. Baptism ritually places a person under the terms of God's peace treaty. Either they will persevere as recipients of the covenant of grace or they will show themselves as those who are covenant-breakers in history and eternity.

So what does discipling the nations look like? If we go back to concepts from chapter 2, in the end would there not be seeming overlap with the family, church, and state, ending in nationally covenanted Christian nations? Over time this would be exactly the case.

What this is not is what Duane Garret argues—that this thinking "implies a Constantinian vision of Christianity, in which the people are to become Christian because the emperor is Christian."[5] He seems to jump to an assumption that representation somehow leads to the furthering of Christendom by the sword and entrance into the church based upon the oath of a civil magistrate. This is a common misconception that is cleared up with the understanding of differing jurisdictions and sanctions discussed in chapter 2.

The sphere of the household differs from that of the state. A man can profess for his household and thereby unite his children to Jesus in the church. An emperor could not do the same. A parent might also use the rod to instruct his child, but he is not sanctioned to use the sword to punish wrongdoing in his neighbor. A church can excommunicate or cut off

5. Duane A. Garrett, "Meredith Kline on Suzerainty, Circumcision, and Baptism," in *Believer's Baptism*, 281.

a member from the body of Christ. An emperor cannot. An emperor can use the sword to execute justice. The church cannot. The common "Constantinian" misunderstanding does not properly distinguish the physical sword from the Sword of the Spirit.

Nations can make covenant with God. In doing so they formally place themselves under the terms of God's Word. It does not, though, happen as some might describe above. Individuals place themselves under God's covenant. These individuals over time become representatives. They become representatives in their households, churches, and communities (as civil magistrates). If this process continued over time, how would it *not* become officially a "Christian nation"?

The only other alternative is a large body of Christians and Christian families living in a civil sphere of so-called neutral laws. Neutrality is impossible individually and as a family. The same is true for a nation. Over time, as more professing believers are representatives in the institutions, the nation begins to conform itself to God's Word. At some point it can be officially designated as a Christian nation on the basis of oaths taken and the laws that have been put in place by God's representatives. This is the process of leavening that Jesus speaks about: "The kingdom of heaven is like leaven that a woman took and hid in three measures of flour, till it was all leavened" (Matt. 13:33). Leavening speaks to the growth of the kingdom. Over time, the process of growth occurs until the whole loaf is ready for the oven.

We have been preaching an abridged gospel, a reduction of Christianity. We have discounted the power of the Holy Spirit this side of heaven. What we need is high-powered evangelism that takes the whole gospel to the whole world. Without the whole gospel and an understanding of institutional growth and success brought about by covenant obedience, we inherently say that the pagans will inherit the earth over time until a time of final judgment when Jesus comes to effect what the Holy Spirit could not do through His church.

This inheritance by the pagan and disinheritance by the godly would be compounding. Think about officially heathen nations. How many missionaries were sent out to the world from the Soviet Union during the previous century? Over time, if we retreat from the world around us (think Canaan), we will be overcome and our soul-saving efforts of an abridged gospel will be stymied. Contrast such a scenario with an attitude of Joshua or Caleb (Num. 13-14). There are giants in what seems to be an evil world, but as we harness the power of another world, preach the gospel, teach the laws of our Great King, and live obediently in covenant with Him, we will witness the promised blessings and see the inheritance promised in His Word. This is the Great Commission. This is the baptism of nations into the name of the Father and of the Son and of the Holy Spirit.

SUMMARY AND CONCLUSION

THERE IS ONE PRIMARY RELATIONSHIP IN this life for all of us. It is the relationship to our Creator God. Even though we cannot see Him directly, this relationship is not magical or mystical. It is not merely an other-worldly, spiritual relationship with no connection to the here and now. It is ethical in nature. It is a legal bond. It is a covenant.

This bond was first established with the first man, Adam. The terms of the original, legal relationship with Adam were broken. This resulted in negative sanctions. Whether it is acknowledged or not, we are born under those sanctions as if we were the very ones who broke the terms. This is called representation. The legal bond is called a covenant. Nothing has changed since the beginning of time in regards to the structure through which God interacts with His creation. He still makes use of these two important realities.

Following the fall of Adam, God immediately began to bring about a plan of redemption for His creation. This plan was carried out through a covenant structure. He made an everlasting covenant with Abraham. In this covenant, Abraham's true descendants are represented by the second Adam, who is Jesus Christ. Jesus sets them back into good standing with their Creator and enables them to keep the terms of the covenant. These true descendants of Abraham are God's people. They have the faith required for salvation.

In time and history on earth we do not possess eyes to see the hearts of men. There have been men and women of faith since the time of Abraham, but God works out His redemptive plan over time. One day His plan will be complete, history will be consummated, and Abraham's true descendants will join their Father and glorify Him for all eternity. But for now God has designed a structure through which to relate to Him and bring about His redemptive plan. It is the covenant.

Every covenant has at least five foundational components. First, there is a supreme authority who is sovereign in the relationship. Second, there is functional subordination or hierarchy through which to carry out and govern the relationship. Third, there are terms or laws by which to operate or conduct the arrangement. Fourth, there are consequences or sanctions, both positive and negative, for conducting oneself in accordance with these laws. And finally, there is future provision or continuity outlined in the relationship.

A covenant is established by an oath. It is the oath that legally binds an individual or institution to the Lord. Being legally bound means that the oath-taker and those he represents are now liable to receive blessings or punishments as stipulated within the terms of the covenant. The person taking the oath is calling on God to carry out the sanctions.

There are three oath-bound institutions established by God through which He works to bring about His purpose in history. Each institution has its own God-given jurisdiction and unique sanctions it can carry out. The three institutions are the family, the church, and the state (civil government). All three are made up of individuals who are under the terms of the covenant at creation referenced above. To understand how God relates to each of these institutions, we must understand the role of representation within the covenant structure.

God is not visible in a direct way on earth, yet in His redemptive plan for creation He still intends to extend His rule through history. Man is given the task of representing Him in this endeavor. He has sovereignly chosen to work through man to carry out His will. Whereas He can act in any way He chooses, He has revealed through His Word that in general He relates in covenant with men acting as covenant representatives. They represent God to men and men to God.

If they are faithful representatives they will carry out the laws of their covenant head. They will represent His character. God's covenant document is His Word as revealed in Scripture. It names the sovereign, His chosen hierarchy, His laws (which are an expression of His character), the sanctions due obedient and disobedient subjects, and a detail of His redemptive plan that includes future continuity or inheritance for His people at the end of time.

Our first representative, Adam, broke the terms of the covenant at creation and we are all under the curse due him for disobedience. In his sinful, depraved state man is at war with God. God offers another covenant in history, which essentially is a peace treaty. This covenant, like the first, offers life to those perfectly obedient to the sovereign. At the same time it requires the death penalty for disobedience to the covenant, broken by the representative head, Adam.

In His grace, God made provision for a sacrifice, paying the penalty and fulfilling the terms of the covenant. The provision made for His people, the elect, was another covenant representative, Christ. In representing His people He has taken on Himself the negative sanctions due them for rebellion against God and enables them to appear before God as justified and redeemed due to the work of Christ in His death and resurrection.

The perfect righteousness of His people is present at the end of history when His people are glorified, but in time and in history they are still imperfect individually. Sin is still present. Christ's definitive work in His death and resurrection took place, but a progressive work is ongoing until the end of time, when the results of His work will be fully realized in the glorification of His saints.

Just as sin and imperfection are present in the lives of God's elect in history, so there is sin and imperfection in the life of His church. His church in history is comprised of all those under the terms of His covenant or treaty. Before the consummation at the end of time, the church in history is imperfect. Some will break the terms of the covenant. God alone knows His people at the consummation of all history. In the meantime He has called out His people, the church.

Under the New Covenant administration He calls men to submit to His rule. Those that persevere and are found faithful are those for whom Christ died. In the meantime, the structure and representation of the church are designed by God to purify it.

This peace treaty is God's redemptive covenant. Following the first advent, the expression of this is the New Covenant. The covenant appoints God as sovereign. It appoints elders to represent the sovereign to the people and the people to the sovereign. It stipulates laws. It also stipulates sanctions. These sanctions are unique to the jurisdiction of the church. Unlike the state, the church cannot execute. Unlike the family, the church cannot make use of the rod. The church's lawful sanction for unrepentant disobedience is excommunication or dismissing subjects from fellowship with God.

Elders are called to represent God on earth in marking out the boundaries of the church. The elders are called to judge rightly. Their decision to excommunicate serves as a warning that covenant-breakers will be cut off from the fellowship of God forever.

In addition to cutting off covenant-breakers from the fellowship, the church is also called to guard the entrance into the covenant. Those gaining entrance into the covenant are set apart judicially based on their confession. Through a man's confession he submits to the rule of his Lord and subjects himself to the terms of God's covenant Word.

This is where one of the other covenant institutions plays a critical role. The family is also a covenant institution bound by God. In marriage, a man and a woman take an oath that binds their relationship before God. This oath creates a legal bond. It is important to note that marriage reflects the covenant made between Jesus and His church. The peace treaty discussed above is the ultimate marriage covenant. The relationship of a man to his wife is merely to be a reflection of this ultimate covenant (Eph. 5).

Scripture states that in general the man is God's representative head in the family. Through his headship he represents the confession of his family. Just as we are damned by Adam's confession and saved by the confession and redemptive work of Jesus, so is a man's family placed in the church in time and in history through the confession of the representative head. A child's confession is made through his head.

As a covenantal unit, the family in general is blessed or cursed based on the confession of the head. This is intuitive. Whereas we all know of stories where God chooses to intervene, we can fully understand this concept. A child who grows up in a household where a genuine fear and love for the Lord is present will in general turn out different from a child who is reared in a God-hating household where physical and emotional abuse is present. We would prefer to believe that in general the lovely little child is spared and only treated as an individual before God, but we know better. The child is treated both as an individual (as we will all be judged) and within the context of a covenant. This is the "one and the many." This is Trinitarian. God is reflected in His creation.

The fact that in the family a representative head's confession is taken for the child is seen clearly in baptism. In the Old Testament circumcision represented inclusion into God's covenant people. A boy in an Israelite family was not circumcised following his own confession but following the confession of his representative head. This is precisely what we see in New Testament baptism. Households were baptized because nothing has been altered in regard to the way God relates to His people on earth. God still relates to people in terms of covenant stipulations and obligations. He still relates to His creation from within the three covenant institutions, each carrying out His will and sanctions in each of their unique jurisdictions.

Some take specific New Covenant texts in Scripture to support an altering of covenant structure on earth following the coming of Christ. They use texts from Jeremiah and Hebrews to support the concept of only the elect being members of the New Covenant. This interpretation discounts the context of the Scriptures as a whole and divorces the concept of covenant from time and history altogether.

Far from being a way God relates to His people in history, those that interpret the texts this way end up reducing God's peace treaty to an other-worldly structure that cannot even be perceived on earth. This is a radical disconnect of material and spiritual, and renders God's peace treaty on earth impotent to carry out His will through His ordained structure on earth.

A close look at the New Covenant texts of Jeremiah and Hebrews reveals a beautiful revelation of the superiority of Christ the mediator and His acceptable sacrifice. Far from being a covenant with only the elect at the end of time, these passages are consistent with passages throughout the New Testament that discuss apostasy from the covenant as a distinct possibility. The covenant is very much a peace treaty offered to rebellious man. Those that keep the terms of the treaty will be clearly revealed at the end of time. Until then, God has placed men to represent Him in the purifying work of the church.

Understanding that God has a plan for His creation is critical in understanding the concept of covenant. God does not just relate to His creation through covenant for the purpose of relating. He relates to His creation through covenant for the express purpose of redeeming what was cursed and bringing glory to Creator God. This is the whole gospel. God not only wants to save the souls of His people, He so loves the world and wants to redeem it.

At the outset man was called to subdue the earth. This command did not change with the curse. It was reiterated in the life of Noah and his family and again with the Great Commission. The redemption of the world was prefigured in the life of Israel, God's Old Testament covenant bride.

Israel was a special people called by God who were given a land to conquer. They were given a land. In following the terms of the covenant with God through subjecting themselves ethically, they would have been able to take the land. Far from taking the land, they repeatedly broke the terms of the covenant and were given a certificate of divorce by their Husband.

Christ took for Himself a new bride. This bride was his people, the church. With the coming of Christ the groom, His saints were given back title to the whole earth. As the archetypical Joshua, Jesus leads His people into the land to take it. They do this just as Israel was to subdue Canaan. They subdue it by conforming ethically to the marriage covenant on earth. The difference is that God has provided His Holy Spirit. As the book of Hebrews makes plain, they have a sacrifice that can now truly take away sins, and at Pentecost they received the power of the Holy Spirit. Their victory in time and in history is sure.

To think otherwise is to question the power of the Holy Spirit. It also discounts the role of representation discussed above. Christ's physical presence is not required for progressive victory throughout history. His presence through His representatives is sufficient. These representatives are present in each of His covenant institutions. As each of these institutions is governed by representatives according to the laws of God, God's rule in history will be extended. This is covenant structure and representation at work. It blankets every area of life.

What needs to be understood more than ever before is that we are living in a time when God's people are turning back to His Word as the law to live by in every area of life. Just as Josiah found God's Word, dusted it off, and began calling God's people to live according to it, God's people today are rediscovering the truth that His Holy Scripture governs every area of life on earth.

God's people are not strangers in a strange land. They are more than conquerors in a land given to them by their Lord God who is sovereign over all creation. What is needed today is a wholesale change in the areas of law and governance for the family, the church, and the state. All of this begins with the conversion of individuals who subject themselves to the laws of God and represent Him in each of these institutions.

As they do, we will begin seeing the fruits of the true gospel flourish. In general, those that subject themselves to the laws of God will be blessed with greater influence and capital over time (if we believe what Scripture says) and will be in the position of inheriting God's creation progressively over time. This is the whole gospel. We are called to spread it. "Go therefore and make disciples of all nations, baptizing them in the name of the Father and of the Son and of the Holy Spirit, teaching them to observe all that I have commanded you" (Matt. 28:19–20). Let us go make disciples and work within the structure designed by our Creator.

Elders are called to represent God in His covenant on earth. They are to guard the called-out church. Fathers, let us confess Christ and represent our households to Him. God give us the grace to represent well Christ to our baptized children of the covenant.

www.ingramcontent.com/pod-product-compliance
Lightning Source LLC
Chambersburg PA
CBHW022007090426
42741CB00007B/922